Preschool
for Parents

What Every Parent Needs to Know
About Preschool

Preschool
for Parents

What Every Parent Needs to Know
About Preschool

Diane Trister Dodge
Toni S. Bickart

Contributing Author:
Cynthia Scherr

Sourcebooks, Inc.
Naperville, IL

Washington, DC

Co-published by:

Teaching Strategies, Inc.
P.O. Box 42243
Washington, DC 20015
(800) 637-3652
FAX: (202) 364-7273

Sourcebooks, Inc.
P.O. Box 4410
Naperville, IL 60567-4410
(630) 961-3900
FAX: (630) 961-2168

Sourcebooks

Internal illustrations by Jennifer Barrett O'Connell
Photo of Diane Trister Dodge by Connie Reider, photo of Toni Bickart by Teaching
Strategies, Inc.

Library of Congress Cataloging-in-Publication Information
Dodge, Diane Trister.
      Preschool for parents: what every parent needs to know about
preschool/Diane Trister Dodge, Toni S. Bickart.
      p.   cm.
      Includes bibliographical references (p.   ) and index.
      ISBN 1-57071-172-0 (alk. paper)
      1. Education, Preschool—United States. 2. Education, Preschool—Parent
participation—United States. 3. School choice—United States. 4. Child development—
United States. 5. Readiness for school—United States.
      I. Bickart, Toni S. II. Title
LB1140.23.D63   1998
372.21—dc21   98-17216
                                                    CIP

Table of Contents

Acknowledgments

Several years ago, Cynthia Scherr suggested that we write a book for parents on how to select a good preschool. She helped us begin this task as she herself searched for a high-quality preschool for her own two children. We are indebted to Cynthia for leading the way and preparing drafts of the first two chapters of this book.

Two other individuals helped us define a direction for this book and dropped other priorities to help us rework many drafts. Our first thanks go to Emily Kohn, who never allows us to get away with an irrelevant thought or unsubstantiated statement. Sybil Wolin read through several drafts, continually reminded us of our message, and pushed us with challenging questions and specific recommendations. Her insights and guidance were invaluable.

Larry Bram kept us on task, encouraged us when we were discouraged, and was instrumental in preparing the appendixes.

We want to acknowledge Jennifer Barrett O'Connell for the illustrations, which came from our book for teachers, *The Creative Curriculum for Early Childhood.*

Several people reviewed the final drafts and offered valuable suggestions. We would like to thank Jim Clay, Monica Vacca, Sharon Yandian, Glenda Davis-Canteen, David Arfin, Daniel Haft, Laura Colker, Brenda Kuvin, Elisabeth Lyons, Joyce Migdal, and Jim Roumell for critiquing our last draft.

Through our partnership with Parent Soup, World Wide Web community, we have had the opportunity to "chat" each week with parents of preschoolers across the country. They continually reminded us of the questions they struggle with in choosing a good program for their child—questions we hope we have answered in this book.

This book is our second venture in copublishing with Sourcebooks, and it has been a pleasure to collaborate with them. We particularly wish to thank Todd Stocke, our editor, and Eileen Primozic, our publicist.

Introduction

The challenge of selecting a preschool for your child is exciting, confusing, and scary all at once. You probably have several alternatives from which to choose, and you may be getting conflicting advice about each of them. For example, you want your child to be academically ready for elementary school. You also want your child to learn, grow, and socialize in a safe, healthy environment with supportive adults, but you may not know how to tell which preschools will make this happen and which will not. At the same time, you have to consider family needs, such as the distance between your home and prospective preschools, schedule, tuition, and perhaps, religious affiliation.

Why We Wrote This Book

The purpose of this book is to give you the information you need to select the right preschool program for your child. While many good books are already available that help you understand different teaching philosophies, compare full-day and part-day options, explain costs, describe the screening process, and provide overviews of the many choices available, we start with a simple truth that organizes this book and all the suggestions we make: *the best preschool teaching practices make the most of children's natural inclination to play.* What's more, you don't have to choose between academic learning and enjoyable play experiences for your children. The idea that you must make a choice is in part due to different definitions. When some people talk about "academics," they may be thinking specifically of teaching children their letters and sounds, numbers, colors, shapes, and so on. Our definition of academics is much broader. Academics should address such questions as:

How do children become literate?

How do children learn to think mathematically and like a scientist?

How do children learn about the world around them?

How do children create through the arts?

Almost all current research on young children clearly indicates that when children play, they learn—and they learn social, emotional, and physical skills as well as academics. Our view that a quality preschool program is one that promotes learning through rich play experiences is based on that research.

About the Book

We begin by identifying some of the practical considerations involved in choosing a preschool and by discussing the basic requirements of good safety and health practices. You can't begin to think about what your child is learning until you feel assured that the preschools you are looking at will keep your child safe and maintain good health practices. We provide a picture of high-quality preschool programs, including how space is used and how children spend their time. We describe how children benefit from an appropriate, well-balanced daily schedule and a well-organized classroom and outdoor environment. Because a program is only as good as its staff, we also want you to know exactly what good teachers do in a quality program.

Next, we focus on the importance of learning—socially and emotionally, physically, and in the academic subject areas. Here we offer our best knowledge on the ways that learning in young children can most effectively be supported and encouraged. We want you to see how children benefit when they learn by doing, when they initiate their own learning, and when they are guided by teachers who understand how children learn through challenging play experiences. We tell you what you *should* see and what you should *not* see when you visit preschools. We offer some questions you can ask the staff and make suggestions for what you can do at home. Finally, we discuss kindergarten, the next big step in your child's education. Because five- and six-year-olds are more like preschoolers than like first graders, we believe, as research suggests and the National Association for the Education of Young Children recommends, that a kindergarten classroom should look more like a preschool than an elementary school. We tell you why and how this information may affect your selection of a preschool.

You can learn a lot by talking with others and interviewing program directors on the phone. However, nothing replaces visiting the program and seeing with your own eyes what classrooms look like and how teachers relate to children. To help you with each of these steps, we provide two checklists you can use for screening and visiting preschools (see appendix C).

This book is based on the work we do as staff developers with preschools, Head Start programs, child care centers, and school systems across the country as well as our own experiences as classroom teachers and parents. It reflects the philosophy and practices we described in our book for teachers, *The Creative Curriculum for Early Childhood*. We hope to arm you with an understanding of what to look for and how to find a high-quality program where your child will be happy, develop important skills, and become excited about learning.

– 1 –
Thinking about Preschool

Sometime after your child's second birthday, you, like many parents, may begin thinking about preschool. You will be faced with deciding what kind of program will be best for your child and who else will influence his or her growth and development. You are not alone in your dilemma. Many parents have questions about what is best and how they can tell what is right for their child.

Questions Parents Ask

What's the best age for my child to start preschool?

How can I be sure my child will be safe, happy, and well cared for?

How can I be sure that my child will get an appropriate amount of attention?

My child plays at home. Shouldn't I look for a preschool where my child will learn important skills and concepts?

What type of program will prepare my child for kindergarten?

What's most important–play or academics?

How do I find out if the teachers are well trained?

These are important questions. The preschool years may be the first time your child ventures into a group program. In addition, preschool experiences lay the foundation for the many years of schooling that lie ahead. Like most parents, you want to choose a program where your child will be happy, have friends, develop self-confidence, and learn whatever is needed to succeed in school.

To make your decision, you need to think about your own child first, including such factors as temperament, interests, special preferences, and particular needs. Think also about what preschool children are like. The program practices we describe in this book are appropriate for children three to five years old. While we recognize that many parents enroll their children in a program at two, an appropriate program for two-year-olds should look very different from one for three- to five-year-olds. (We provide an overview of developmental characteristics of two- to five-year-olds in appendix A.)

You will find that all preschool programs are not the same. The classroom and outdoor environment, the ways teachers work with children, and the experiences they offer can differ widely, and these differences can have a profound effect on your child. So the question remains, how do you decide which preschool is best for your child, taking into consideration your child's age and level of maturity?

Just as you choose a health professional who is knowledgeable about and experienced in best practices, or a builder whose craftsmanship is superb, you want your child to have teachers who are knowledgeable about best practices in early childhood education. Good programs are based on accepted theories of child development and the latest validated research on effective instructional approaches.

Once you have this information, you can start to identify the right preschool program for your child. We suggest that a good way to begin is to examine some practical considerations: location, costs, and the like. After you have identified programs in your own area, you will probably want to make a few phone calls to screen programs and narrow your search. Most important of all, you can then plan some visits. Obviously, all the references, phone calls, and public relations literature in the world will not tell you as much as an on-site visit. Use your intuition as well as the information we provide to become both knowledgeable and selective.

Practical Considerations

Many practical considerations will influence your search for the right preschool for your child. You probably have a number of questions and issues to balance, such as what type of program you want, whether you need a part-day or full-day program, how far you are willing to travel, and what you can afford to pay.

Type of program. There may be a variety of choices including nursery schools, co-op preschools, child care programs, public schools, Head Start, and family child care. The best practices we describe in this book can be found in many different types of settings.

Schedule. Think about whether you want a preschool that is part-day or full-day, five days a week or just a few days, during the school year or year-round, and whether you will need extended-hours care. If you are a working parent, a preschool with extended hours and a year-round schedule will be very important. Even for parents who do not work outside the home, a school that is a distance from home and has a three-hour morning session with no extended care may present logistical problems.

Location. You may prefer a school close to your home, close to your place of work, or someplace in-between. This is a more important consideration than it may appear at first glance. If your child has to get up extra early, get ready for school, and ride a long distance every morning, she may arrive at school too wound up or exhausted to enjoy learning and playing—and eventually you will begin to feel stress.

Tuition. Some states fund preschool programs for which no tuition is charged. In other cases, tuition may range from 100 percent federal subsidies for families that qualify for Head Start programs to thousands of dollars for preschools that route children to private preparatory schools. To maintain a diverse student body, many schools offer tuition assistance or sliding fee scales for lower income parents. In addition to tuition, other fees may be involved: registration fees, materials fees, field trip expenses, and after-hours fees. Many schools also have high penalties if you arrive late to pick up your child (schools often use this tactic to remind parents that it is traumatic for a child to be the last one left at school—as well as inconsiderate of the teacher's schedule). Some schools require a full year's tuition in advance or a commitment for one year's enrollment. Cancellation policies vary as well, depending on how much of the school year your child completes. For many parents, part of the cost of child care is tax deductible.

Religious affiliation. You may consider religious education to be your family's responsibility alone; you may want the values of your religion reinforced through the preschool experience; or you may want to rule out preschools with any sort of connection to religion. Churches and synagogues often subsidize or support preschools in their facilities, both to provide a much-needed service to the community and to further the mission of the institution.

Beginning the Search

How do you find out about the preschools in your area? Whether or not you are new to an area, you will probably want to use several methods of getting referrals. Keep in mind that everyone has different criteria for selecting a preschool. Never take a recommendation at face value. Screen and visit the school yourself. You know what will work for your child and your family. We list below a number of good services for beginning your search. (See appendixes E and F for contact information.)

Word of mouth. Perhaps the easiest way to find a preschool is to get recommendations from families whose family values and views about education are similar to yours. Ask your friends with young children. Talk to parents of slightly older children as well—they've been through their child's preschool experience fairly recently and may have very helpful advice. Ask your pediatrician, your colleagues at work, the children's librarian, other parents you meet at the park or playground, or leaders or members of your religious community.

Elementary schools. Most elementary schools will know the preschools that their kindergartners attended. Indeed, many schools run preschool programs of their own. Whether public or private, the elementary schools near you are a good place to start for referrals. Call the principal, go to the school's open house, or attend a school fair to find out about area preschools.

Churches/Synagogues. Many religious institutions run preschools or rent space to preschools. Sometimes the preschool is an integral part of the institution, and sometimes it is completely separate. Do not assume that the preschool in the Presbyterian Church is just for Presbyterian children; most preschools based in religious institutions welcome children from the community at large. You will have to assess the program and determine whether it is compatible with your beliefs and values.

Community centers. Community centers often have bulletin boards or other means of circulating information. Sometimes the director can refer you to a nearby preschool. If your community or neighborhood has a newsletter, read it for preschool advertisements.

Employer-based resource and referral. If you work for a large company, you may have access to resource and referral services through your employer. Many companies contract with resource and referral agencies to provide child care and preschool information to employees. Check and see if you are eligible for this benefit.

Office of Child Development/Department of Health and Human Services. Usually one of these two state offices (the names vary state-by-state) is responsible for licensing preschool programs in your state. Find which one provides this service and call. Most states regulate preschools, and the licensing body in your state can give you a list of licensed preschools near you. You can also obtain a compliance history of one or more schools in which you may be interested.

NACCRRA. The National Association of Child Care Resource and Referral Agencies can help you locate preschool and child care programs in your area. NACCRRA has chapters in all fifty states and can refer you to the appropriate resource person in your area. Call them at 1-800-424-2246.

YMCA/JCC. Many Young Men's Christian Associations or Jewish Community Centers have preschools and extended-hour care programs. They may also be able to refer you to the preschools they know of in your area. Check the telephone book for a local number.

NAEYC. The National Association for the Education of Young Children accredits center-based early education and care programs that meet standards of quality. For a list of accredited programs near you, call 1-800-424-2460 or visit their website (see appendix F).

NAFCC. The National Association for Family Child Care is a membership organization that also accredits family child care homes. Most quality family child care providers offer a preschool curriculum. To find out which family child care homes near you meet their standards, call 1-800-359-3817.

Yellow pages. The yellow pages in your telephone book will at least give you an idea of the range of preschools available in your area. Check several categories: preschools, schools, private schools, child care, family child care. You may be able to narrow the field of possible preschools if location is extremely important. You can also make a list of possibilities and then ask people you know about the reputation of the different schools.

Parent/child/family publications. Check the family-oriented publications in your area. Sometimes they are distributed free at local bookstores or coffee shops. Preschools may advertise or contribute articles to these publications. Look for the education column in your local newspaper; the education columnists may also be familiar with area preschools.

The Screening Phone Call

Screening preschools by phone will help you narrow the number of places that you think are worth a visit. Sometimes you will be able to tell with one phone call whether or not a school is for you and your child. When you call, ask to speak with the director. Beyond the practical issues, ask questions that will help give you a sense of whether or not the program meets your needs.

You will probably want to start with administrative questions first, because you may not need to continue the conversation if, for example, the schedule and tuition don't meet your needs. Licensing and regulations will vary from state to state since each has different regulations. Check with the National Association of Resource and Referral Agencies (1-800-424-2246) to find out who the regulating body is in your state. Appendix C has a list of suggested questions for your screening phone call.

Don't be shy about asking a lot of questions. Good directors welcome in-depth questions because they show that you will be a concerned, involved parent–and these are the best types of parents to have. Good teachers also like talking about their work and sharing their enthusiasm for their profession. Your questions show that you value their influence on your child's life.

If you are satisfied with the answers you get to these initial questions, ask the school to send you an information booklet and schedule a visit. You will want to see for yourself the classroom your child would attend so you can decide whether you think the school is right for him or her. You may be very impressed by a conversation with the administrator of a preschool and a tour of the facilities, but if the teacher of the three-year-old classroom is cold and perfunctory and the children appear more whiny than happy, the atmosphere in the room may discourage you from sending your child there. A director can have the best of intentions, but if the staff have not internalized the philosophy of the program, you won't want your child there.

When you visit potential preschool programs, there are three essential elements to consider: safety, health practices, and the staff. We cover these topics in the next chapter.

– 2 –
First Things First

Your first and most important consideration is whether your child will be safe and well cared for. This means that a preschool has to meet standards for safety, for healthy practices, and for staff who know what they are doing. This chapter provides information on how to evaluate these three factors in your visits to preschools.

Safety–Indoors and Out

Safety is a number one issue in selecting a preschool. A safe environment encourages exploration and discovery without inhibiting children's curiosity.

Looking Indoors

Sufficient space for children's play and activities is clearly the first thing you will want to notice as you check for a safe environment. Each state has different minimum space requirements for the number of children served. (Your local resource and referral organization can give you this information. Call Child Care Aware at 1-800-424-2246 to find the resource and referral agency closest to you.) However, minimum requirements are usually not sufficient. The National Association for the Education of Young Children

(NAEYC) recommends at least thirty-five square feet of usable indoor space per child.

A safe environment is well planned. It includes clear traffic paths so children don't get in each other's way, exits and escape paths that are easy to see and free from any obstructions, doors that can be opened from both inside and out, and floor covering (when used) that does not slip, is nonflammable and nontoxic, and is in good repair.

A safe environment is well equipped. It includes special safety items such as clearly visible fire extinguishers, first aid kits that are appropriately stocked, and properly functioning smoke detectors. Materials and equipment should be in good repair. You should see a written evacuation and/or contingency plan posted somewhere in the room.

A safe environment has certain other characteristics as well. Electrical outlets are protected and wires located away from traffic areas. Furniture that children use is sturdy, clean, and child sized. Stairs and hallways are well lit. In the bathroom, steps and footstools are nonslip and appropriately sized. Ask whether all paint and other materials children use are lead free and nontoxic. You should not see any chemical cleaning supplies around, because they are locked up away from children.

Looking Outdoors

Outdoor space should be organized to prevent accidents. The space should be enclosed and designed so that children are always visible. Look for grass, wood chips, or other cushioning materials under climbing equipment, swings, and slides, and observe to see that outdoor equipment is securely anchored and that there is enough space between structures to prevent collisions. If there is a sandbox, it should be covered when not in use to keep out cats and other animals who might use it as a litter box.

Health–Daily Habits and Nutrition

Preschool children may still be learning the basics of sharing their toys, their snacks, and their blankets, but one thing they already know how to share is a cold, fever, or flu. The more exposure to other children they have, the more likely they are to get sick. While you can expect your child to get many childhood communicable diseases, practices that keep children as healthy as possible should be evident in the preschool environment.

Look for adequate ventilation and lighting, a comfortable temperature, and sanitary conditions. Some sanitary conditions we think are especially important include evidence of frequent handwashing (for example, before and after eating, after using the toilet, and after handling classroom pets), plenty of soap and tissues, and children using their own bedding at rest periods.

Good nutrition is another aspect of promoting wellness in young children. Look for a preschool that encourages healthy eating habits and is aware of children's nutritional needs. As you know, attitudes about food develop early in life and are difficult to change. The foods children eat affect their well-being, physical growth, ability to learn, and overall behavior. Eating moderately, eating a variety of foods, and eating in a pleasant, relaxed atmosphere all help young children form healthy habits. If your visit includes staying at the program during a meal or snack time, you will want to take special note that the food is served in a calm manner.

Staff–The Foundation of the Program

A program is only as good as its staff. The people who teach and care for your child are more important than school names, location, tuition, equipment, supplies, or philosophy. You need to be able to assess a teacher's style and philosophy, training and experience, and unfortunately, you need to consider unpleasant topics such as child abuse, too.

You want a teacher who will get to know your child individually. Some days your child may be in a quiet or shy mood and may just want to curl up in a cozy place and read books. Another day, he or she may be exuberant with energy and may want to find something active to do, even when it is time to be indoors. A flexible and creative teacher will structure the right learning experiences for your child.

The most important single characteristic of good teaching practice is the quality of teachers' interaction with children. For example, you might see teachers showing affection by touching a child's shoulder, having children in their laps, or kneeling to speak to a child at his or her eye level. Children cannot learn if they are not well cared for. Young children live in the moment; when they have hurt feelings or bodies, they need a responsive adult right away. As a parent, you would not dream of ignoring your crying child; you want a teacher who will offer the same degree of comfort and security. Children need to know that school is a safe, caring place for them to learn.

Good teachers know how to build on children's interests to guide and facilitate their learning. For example, if your child shows interest in the box of magnets on Wednesday, his teacher might suggest that he walk around the room with the large magnet and see what sticks to it. Then she might ask him some open-ended questions about what he observed; for example, "What did you find out? Did you notice anything about the things that stick to the magnet?" Young children then learn they can make important discoveries through exploration.

A good indication of the quality of the staff is how long teachers have been with the program and whether ongoing training is provided. Teachers who are well trained and experienced are more likely to have the characteristics we describe throughout this book. You need not hesitate to ask how the school hires new teachers and what characteristics the director values most.

Finally, we must mention the distressing topic of child abuse. As a parent, you have to be aware that this can occur. Some preschools require a criminal records check and a clearance from child protective services. After you have confirmed that staff members have been appropriately screened, you have to use your own good judgment. If you have any doubts or suspicions—if anything does not seem right—too many children, places in which children cannot be seen, a strict discipline policy, a no drop-in visits policy—do not send your child to that school.

What You Should See When You Visit

There are some basic indicators which will reassure you that the program takes children's safety and health seriously. In addition, take time to to observe the staff and ask a few questions.

The Environment

- Classroom and outdoor areas are free from conditions that might cause accidents.

- Materials and equipment are child-size and in good repair.

- Written procedures are posted for dealing with emergencies such as fires or accidents.

- Soap and paper towels are located where children can easily reach them to wash their hands.

The Teachers

Observe how teachers interact with the children. Think about your own child and imagine how he or she would respond to the adults in the classroom. You should see teachers who:

- Supervise children at all times, indoors and outdoors.

- Serve nutritious and well-balanced snacks and meals, create a relaxed atmosphere, and avoid pressuring children to eat everything.

- Show respect for children's ideas and feelings: "That's an interesting idea. I never thought of that before," or "I can see that you are angry. Tell me about it so I can help."

- Respond to children's questions and requests and call children by name: "Evan, let's look at our picture schedule so you can see for yourself what we do after snack."

- Provide all children with the same opportunities to participate in the program: "Sarah can't run like you can, but we can find a way for her to play the game also."

What You Should *Not* See

- Long open spaces that tempt children to run indoors.

- Equipment in poor repair or obvious hazards on the playground.

- More children per adult than the staff seems to be able to handle.

- The use of food to reward or punish children.

- Teachers who raise their voices in anger or regularly call across the room to children.

- Teachers handling children roughly or without respect.

Questions to Ask

- How often do you have fire drills?

- Are members of your staff trained in CPR and pediatric first aid?

- What is your policy regarding sick children?

- Do you provide meals and snacks or do you expect families to provide food for each child?

- How do you accommodate children with restricted diets?

- What is your policy about releasing children at the end of the day?

- What in your opinion makes a good teacher?

- In what ways do teachers communicate with parents?

Once you know that a preschool program meets your standards for keeping your child safe and healthy, and that the teachers are well trained, knowledgeable, and nurturing, you can think about how your child will learn. The next chapter describes the best route to learning for preschool children.

– 3 –
Play Is Children's Work

Like many parents, you may wonder if a program that focuses on academics is better than one that emphasizes learning through play. It's unfortunate that people too often take polarized positions on this issue. Some who recognize the importance of play feel it is inappropriate to push academics. Others believe that children will fall behind if they are not taught academics at a young age. We believe this either/or thinking misses the point and does not reflect current knowledge.

Contrary to what one might expect, the benefits of rich play experiences during the preschool years are extensive and address academic goals for reading and writing, math, science, social studies, and the arts. Several decades of research show that high-quality preschool programs that aim to strengthen social and emotional skills through play have positive effects on all aspects of children's development—including cognitive or intellectual development. What's more, these positive effects are long lasting. Programs that overemphasize academic learning through teacher-directed instruction in preschool may produce short-term results, but they fail in the long run to improve children's success in school and in life. Research has focused on two important benefits: emotional well-being and cognitive development.

Emotional well-being. Children in programs where they can select activities and pursue their interests and ideas show lower levels of stress than do children in programs that are more teacher directed. The first approach is described as "child-directed" or "child-initiated" learning. The contrasting approach, which educators call "teacher-directed" instruction, is associated with more stress behaviors in children, especially during group times and workbook activities.[1] In addition, children in programs that emphasize child-initiated learning have higher expectations for their own success, are less dependent on adult approval, and are more willing to attempt challenging academic tasks than children in teacher-directed programs.[2]

Cognitive development. Research also shows that a strong emphasis on academics and teacher-directed instruction is not necessary for children to learn academic skills. In fact, preschool and kindergarten children in classrooms that encourage child-initiated learning have better language skills, do better in math and science,[3] and score higher on measures of creativity and divergent thinking skills than do children in other kinds of programs.[4]

Why should this be the case? In high-quality preschool programs, teachers understand child development and how children learn best. They capitalize on children's naturally developing capabilities rather than forcing the development of skills. Good teachers understand what is involved in learning academic subjects and recognize that the preschool years are the prime time for children to learn through their play.

Learning through Play

When children play, they take the initiative–choosing where they want to play, coming up with ideas, and trying them out. However, this does not mean that teachers do nothing but move around and watch. Rather, teachers have an important role in helping children learn through play.

Teachers set the stage for children's learning by selecting materials they know will engage children and organizing materials effectively in interest areas. They provide guidance if children need help and ask questions to spark children's thinking while allowing and encouraging children to experience the power of feeling in charge of their own learning. In any one play period, your child might choose to work on a puzzle, build a block tower, look through a familiar book and retell the story, and play a game with a friend. When children are free to follow their interests, learning happens naturally. For example, let's look at the learning that occurs as children play with blocks.

WHEN CHILDREN:	THEY ARE LEARNING TO:
Balance one large block on top of another	Control and coordinate small muscles
Place blocks of the same size together	Classify and sort objects by size, shape, and function
Experiment to see how high they can stack blocks until the pile falls	Predict cause-and-effect relationships
Judge how many blocks are needed to fill a space	Estimate and use addition and subtraction

Building with blocks is one of the many ways children learn through play. But, for learning to take place, children must have a variety of materials from which to select, time to use these materials as they choose, and a teacher who appreciates and guides their learning through play.

Types of Play

According to Dr. Sara Smilansky, there are four different types of play. Each one contributes to a child's development and learning.[5]

Functional play involves learning about the physical characteristics of objects. When children explore and examine the functions and properties of objects by pushing and pulling, banging and dropping, they are learning how things feel, taste, smell, and sound, and what they do.

The goal of functional play is to heighten curiosity and motivate children to learn more. In the preschool years, children's curiosity grows. They are motivated to learn more when they have an interesting and challenging environment filled with materials and objects that attract them and inspire their explorations.

WHEN CHILDREN:	THEY ARE LEARNING TO:
Put pegs in a pegboard	Coordinate the actions of their eyes and hands, necessary for reading
Rake sand and make piles	Identify physical characteristics of materials, central to all learning
Float objects in water and see which objects sink or float	Predict and recognize cause and effect relationships, important in science

Constructive play emerges as children gain more experience playing with materials and begin to construct things. For example, when children have explored how blocks feel, how they compare in weight and size, and how they can be used, they begin to use blocks to build something purposeful, such as a road or a house. Or, after exploring the properties of sand, children may begin to use the sand to make a castle, a tunnel, or a birthday cake.

WHEN CHILDREN:	THEY ARE LEARNING TO:
Use blocks and wooden animals to create a zoo	Recreate experiences they have had to better understand them, which is social studies
Make a birthday cake out of sand	Use objects to represent something else, which involves abstract thinking
Gather paper, scissors, and glue for a project	Plan and carry out a task, important for all learning

Games with rules involve children in yet another kind of play. Everyone must understand and agree to the rules for the game to be successful. The younger the child, the more simple the rules need to be. Games with rules help children concentrate, understand limits, and control their behavior to conform to the rules.

Pretend or dramatic play emerges in the toddler years as imitation; it blossoms during the preschool years. Children love playing "make-believe." Think about the times you have seen your child acting and sounding just like you do: pretending to drive a car and making comments like yours; "reading" a book and holding it just like you do; telling a cranky "baby" to behave in your tone of voice.

Children use their imaginations to take on a role and reenact what they have experienced. They play out that role with real or pretend objects. Thus, to pretend, children must recall past experiences, select the aspects that are relevant, and use gestures and words to convince others that they are playing the role "correctly." These are high-level intellectual tasks.

Many research findings indicate that there is a direct relationship between the ability to pretend and children's academic success.[6] When children pretend, they create pictures in their minds and use symbols to represent real objects or events. Why is this important? When they are older and study history, literature, science, and math, they go through the same steps of constructing mental images and using symbols to represent reality. For example, to understand history, students must be able to visualize in their minds what life was like in the past and how events are related. To solve a math problem, they have to create a mental picture of the problem so they know whether to add, subtract, multiply, or divide. Many learning tasks require the ability to visualize and determine alternative ways to consider an issue or answer a question. For this reason, learning to use the imagination during the preschool years, is critical to children's learning in the future.

In summary, research, common sense, and experience bear out the importance of engaging children in active learning—or play.

Brain Research—What We Now Know

Today, we can actually see that when children are active learners—handling materials and trying to figure out how to solve a problem—connections are being made in the brain. Within the last decade, scientists have made exciting breakthroughs in understanding how the human brain develops and works. New brain-imaging technologies, such as magnetic resonance imaging (MRI), enable us to watch brain activity as it takes place.

You have probably noticed an increasing number of articles on brain research in newspapers and magazines as well as stories on TV and radio. Some of the research findings are particularly relevant to parents and teachers of young children. This information supports the approaches we describe throughout the book and may help you select the best preschool program for your child.[7]

- The early years are critical for brain development. By age ten, the brain has formed most of the connections it will use throughout life. Nurturing, supportive, and consistent relationships early in life "wire the brain" for learning and loving.

- The brain actually builds itself. Each sensory experience—what a child sees, hears, touches, tastes, and smells—creates connections (synapses) between brain cells. Repeated experiences solidify these connections and promote understanding.

- The brain is most receptive to learning language during the first ten years of life. The more language a child hears, the greater the child's vocabulary.

- Learning comes through the senses, and language develops in the context of meaningful interactions with adults and other children. The more senses involved, the more solid the learning. Words (like "dog") have meaning because they evoke images in the mind (what a dog looks like, sounds like, smells like, and how it feels to the touch). Direct experiences–connected with the words to describe these experiences–create solid images and understanding, which are essential for success in reading.

- Movement is critical to brain activity. When the hands are active, the brain is more engaged. Therefore, "hands-on" learning–building with blocks, drawing and painting, fitting puzzles together, exploring materials, acting out an experience–actually activates the brain.

- Stress caused by physical or emotional trauma produces a hormone called cortisol. This chemical actually kills off the connections between brain cells in the part of the brain that is important to learning and memory. Too much stress literally "shuts down" the brain. Children can handle stress when they have established positive relationships with their parents and other significant adults, such as teachers.

- Music enhances brain development, especially spatial orientation and the ability to think mathematically. A good time to encourage music experiences is during the preschool years.

Best practice in early childhood education reflects what we have learned from brain research. The active, sensory, movement experiences that are characteristic of preschool children's play actually build the brain.

Multiple Intelligences—How Is Your Child Smart?

In the past, good preschools have always given children opportunities to explore learning in many different ways. Now we have additional research that shows the value of child-initiated learning and validates that children learn as they play.

Dr. Howard Gardner, a Professor of Education at Harvard University, has studied the development of cognitive abilities in human beings and has concluded that people are smart in different ways.[8] Rather than viewing intelligence as a score on a standardized test—which focuses on math and language—he has defined intelligence as the abilities to solve problems that one encounters in real life and to make something or offer a service that society values. Gardner developed a way of classifying human abilities and has identified at least eight different kinds of intelligence in his ongoing research. Each of us has these abilities to some degree but in varying amounts. (Note that only the first two have traditionally been a part of IQ tests.)

Think about your own child. What strengths and interests are you beginning to notice? See how these relate to the different kinds of intelligence we describe.

- Does your child love to talk, ask questions, make up stories, or repeat stories and poems you have read together? This behavior demonstrates *linguistic intelligence*—the ability to use language to express ideas, tell a story, understand others, or learn new vocabulary or a second language with ease.

- Some children particularly enjoy manipulative materials that involve making and repeating patterns, find it easy to divide up a set of objects, or enjoy guessing what caused something to happen. Actions like these highlight *logical/mathematical intelligence*—the ability to understand the system of numbers, add and take away, use one-to-one correspondence, and predict what will happen.

- Children who can listen to music and remember the tune easily may be demonstrating *musical intelligence*. This is the ability to produce and recognize songs, repeat rhythms and chants, and keep a beat.

- Does your child love to build with blocks, make collages and three-dimensional structures, or can he or she easily find your car in a large parking lot? These characteristics may indicate a preference for *spatial intelligence*—the ability to form a mental image of a building or find one's way around a neighborhood.

- Children who are natural athletes, graceful dancers, or seem to learn new concepts by experiencing them using their bodies demonstrate *bodily/kinesthetic intelligence*. This is the ability to manipulate objects skillfully and use the body to solve problems.

- Does your child find it easy to make friends, recognize how others feel, and know how to solve a conflict? This behavior indicates *interpersonal intelligence*—the ability to understand and interact effectively with other people—to "read" emotions and respond appropriately.

- Some children seem able to talk about feelings, express emotions, and carry out their plans in very focused ways. Strengths like these are characteristic of *intrapersonal intelligence*—the ability to understand oneself and to use this knowledge to plan and be self-directed.

- Then there are children who love the outdoors, collect living things to bring indoors, and ask for and look through books to learn the names of different plants and animals. This behavior demonstrates *naturalistic intelligence*—the ability to recognize different kinds of plants or animals in the environment.

Gardner's theory of *multiple intelligences* emphasizes the importance of learning experiences that respect individual interests and build on children's strengths. It encourages teachers and parents to look at each child and ask, "How is this child smart?" rather than "How smart is this child?" When children have opportunities to play with different materials and initiate exploration in ways that are comfortable, they find their own strengths. When children have opportunities to learn through their strengths, they develop confidence in their own abilities.

Emotional Intelligence–More Important Than IQ

Emotional intelligence or IQ–which is more important? With the rush to get children into academic learning today, it appears that many people value a high IQ over emotional well-being and social skills. The research, however, requires us to broaden our view.

The term "emotional intelligence" was first coined in 1990 by psychologists Peter Salovey at Yale and John Mayer at the University of New Hampshire. Since that time, Daniel Goleman, a psychologist and science writer for the *New York Times*, pulled together a decade's worth of research on the topic and wrote a book entitled *Emotional Intelligence*.[9] He describes numerous studies that show emotional intelligence is a better predictor of success in school and in life than is IQ.

Emotional intelligence is defined as the ability to understand one's feelings, control impulses and anger, soothe anxiety, show empathy and interact positively with others, and persevere to achieve one's goals. Is preschool the time and the place to begin building these characteristics? Absolutely. In fact, some research shows that the quality of a child's social skills by age five accurately predicts social and academic competence in later grades.[10] As you might expect, the foundation for emotional intelligence is built in early childhood. Children learn to trust others when adults respond to their needs promptly and sensitively. When adults tune into what children are feeling and use words to describe these feelings, they help children recognize feelings in themselves and others. Children learn by watching and imitating important adults in their lives.

Becoming smart about feelings and developing the ability to control impulses and anger are as important to your child's success in life as constantly hearing language and being exposed to books is to success in reading. Emotional intelligence can be taught, and it is an important goal in every good preschool program. When teachers are responsive, empathetic, and model caring and respectful interactions, they are teaching emotional intelligence.

Looking Ahead

We hope this chapter has given you a perspective for determining what kind of preschool will be best for your child. Understanding the latest research can help you assess the different programs available in your area.

In the remainder of the book, we're going to describe what you should see in a great preschool program—one in which teachers appreciate the power of play in stimulating children's learning. We'll look first at the structure of a program—how space and time are organized for children. Next we'll focus on how excellent preschools strengthen children's social and emotional skills. We will also describe how good preschool programs can enhance children's physical development. Then, in separate chapters, we'll discuss how children explore reading and writing, discover mathematical relationships, work as scientists, research social studies, and create through the arts. Finally, we'll add our thoughts about kindergarten—the next big step in your child's education.

– 4 –

Structure–
Every Child Needs It

For play to result in purposeful and productive learning, the class-room environment and daily program must be structured to achieve this goal. A chaotic setting confuses children and makes it difficult for them to know what to expect and how to behave. Alternatively, a clear structure helps children feel secure and enables them to build social and emotional skills as they learn through their play.

There are two aspects to an effective preschool structure; each is based on a knowledge of child development and how children learn. The first form of structure is the physical environment. A preschool classroom should be organized into distinct interest areas so that children learn to make choices and initiate their own activities. Each interest area offers a different type of learning experience, thus accommodating a variety of learning styles.

A second form of structure is how time is organized. A schedule that offers a good balance of activities and is predictable enables children to know what to expect and helps them feel secure. Children learn to move easily and confidently from one activity to another and to feel in control.

Space—The Physical Environment

Environment affects everyone. Physical surroundings affect how people feel, how comfortable they are, how they relate to others, and how successfully they accomplish what they set out to do. For young children, the environment is particularly important. Because preschoolers learn best through their interactions with objects, materials, and people, the physical environment should serve as the setting for learning. Children in a well-organized environment are able to:

- trust and cooperate with others

- develop independence, make choices, and cleanup

- focus on what they are doing and stay involved in their work

- acquire skills and concepts as they select and use materials

What does a well-organized environment looks like? Imagine yourself entering a preschool classroom for four-year-olds as a visitor.

As you look around the room, you hear a steady hum of activity. You see a teacher kneeling down and talking with several children at the water table. She has asked a question, and the children are busy filling and emptying different size containers. Three children are working in the block area—one by herself, and two others seem to be building a tower together. A book showing pictures of tall buildings is open nearby. Another teacher is in the art area with four children. Two are painting at easels and talking together while two other children are seated and pounding playdough. This teacher is talking with them about the "cookies" they are making. In the house corner, four children are wearing hospital garb. One is a doctor, another a nurse, a third is a clown who visits sick children, and the fourth is the mother of the patient, a doll. They are discussing how to cheer the child who will have surgery tomorrow. Two children are huddled together on pillows in the library area giggling over a book, while two other children are sitting together in front of a computer taking turns and talking about what they are trying to do.

The preschool children in this classroom are involved learners, engaging in activities that interest them. Clearly defined, well-equipped interest areas promote their ability to learn through play.

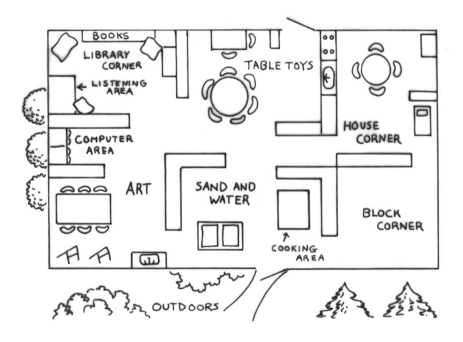

Some programs may call interest areas by different names. Others may not have as many areas as are described here. Generally speaking, programs for younger preschoolers have fewer distinct areas than programs for older children, because younger children do better with fewer choices. And many of the activities we describe—such as cooking, music, and movement—can take place even without a designated area. Here is an overview of interest areas you might expect to see when you visit high-quality preschools.

Blocks: In this area you will see large hardwood unit blocks, arranged by size and shape, with labels on the shelf to show children where each type belongs. Props such as cars, signs, and train tracks inspire children to make towers, bridges, buildings, shopping centers, train stations, and cities. You might also see hollow blocks for building large structures if space allows.

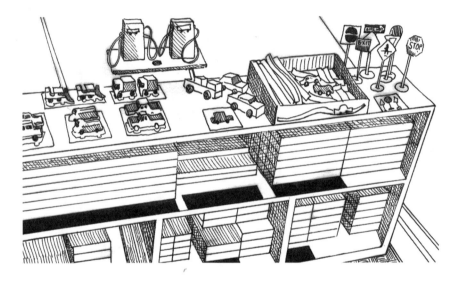

House Corner or Dramatic Play: An assortment of props and equipment invites children to try out different roles. Sometimes the area may be a home with a stove, refrigerator, sink, table, cradles, and beds; at other times, the area may be something else, such as a post office or grocery store, with appropriate props.

Art: In this area are easels, paints, markers, crayons, chalks, glue, scissors, playdough and clay, and cleanup materials. Here children draw, cut, paste, mold, and paint.

Table Toys: Puzzles, games, and small manipulative materials encourage children to sort, classify, make patterns, match, and experiment with construction.

Sand and Water: Here children sift sand and scoop water, build sand castles and blow bubbles, and explore why some objects sink and others float.

Library: This is the primary location for books, writing materials, and in some cases, tape recorders. Here children look through books, listen to recorded stories and music, and write or dictate their own stories or songs.

Music and Movement: Musical instruments, tapes or CDs, and supplies for musical activities invite children to make and listen to music and explore different body movements during the day. There may not be a separate area for these activities.

Cooking: Cooking activities may occur in any area of the room where there is a table and access to water. Working independently or in a small group, children prepare food and eat it. They use bowls, cups, spoons, and other equipment and tools as necessary.

Computers: Some but not all preschools have computers. Two computers are better than one so that computer play can be done as a shared activity. If the software is interactive and encourages preschoolers to experiment, this is a place they can make designs, solve problems, and play games on their own or with others.

Indoor Climbing, Building, and Riding Area: Some preschools are fortunate enough to have space for large equipment indoors, perhaps in a separate room. Such equipment may include a climbing apparatus, slides, a balance beam, large cars and trucks, tricycles, wagons, and scooters.

Outdoors or Playground: Open space and climbing and riding equipment encourage children to run, throw balls, enjoy the outdoors, and socialize. In good weather, many indoor activities can take place outdoors as well.

Organization of Materials

Although each interest area has its own particular materials and equipment, certain characteristics are common to all areas.

A variety of learning materials is available in each interest area so that no matter how children choose to play there, they learn. This means that in the block area, for example, children find props to extend their block activities—farm animals, toy vehicles, signs, flags, books about construction, and writing materials to make signs. The sand and water tables have materials for weighing, measuring, and pouring, as well as funnels, rakes, sieves, sifters, and strainers.

The materials in each interest area are easily accessible so children can find and use them independently, do projects on their own, and put the materials away on low shelves when they are finished playing. Duplicates of many materials and toys reduce the need for sharing, especially for young preschoolers.

The choices are clear so that children will not be overwhelmed. Shelves are neat and uncluttered, with materials carefully displayed and easy to see and find.

Similar materials are grouped together in a logical way to give children the message that teachers expect them to respect and take care of the materials in the classroom. In addition, a clear organizational scheme sets the stage for learning the skills of sorting and classifying. There are picture labels on containers and shelves so children know where materials belong. Being able to find, use, and then cleanup materials independently develops children's sense of competence. Children's private space—a cubby, shelf, or other storage unit—should be clearly marked with their picture and name.

Displays in the classroom show children's work rather than only commercial posters. When children's work is prominently displayed in the classroom, they know their work is important and valued.

Time—A Balanced Day

Organizing the day for preschoolers requires not only careful use of space but also thoughtful planning and a schedule. You may find it difficult to consider putting away coats, telling stories, singing songs, eating snacks, and playing on swings as a schedule, but it is—and it is very important for your preschooler. The schedule forms the basic structure for each day and supports the educational goals for your child. In addition, a daily schedule helps children feel secure and independent and allows them to move from one activity to another easily and confidently. When the schedule suits the developmental and individual needs of the children, it makes the day go more smoothly and enjoyably for everyone.

A good schedule for young children offers a balance between the following types of activities:

- Active and quiet times

- Large group activities, small group activities, and time to play alone or with others

- Indoor and outdoor play times

- Time for children to select their own activities and time for teacher-directed activities

The Importance of Consistency—and Flexibility

Consistency is an important characteristic of the daily schedule. A similar schedule every day lets children know what will happen next. Young children feel secure when they can predict the sequence of events and have some control over their day. They love to remind the teacher that "snack time comes next" or to tell a visitor that "we go outside now."

In a quality preschool, teachers help children anticipate the schedule. As a result, each part of the day—arrival, circle time, transitions, work time, meal times, rest time, and departure—becomes a secure routine for children. Many classrooms use a picture schedule like the one shown on the next page. You may see the schedule drawn on one strip of paper so children can "read" it from left to right. After a few months, children can even tell their teacher or a visitor what they are supposed to do next!

A schedule, however, need not be inflexible. When there is something special for the children to do, good teachers adjust the daily routine. For example, a snow flurry can interrupt class plans so that the children can go outside with pieces of black paper to catch snowflakes and observe their characteristics. Similarly, if an activity is especially successful or engrossing, there's no reason to stop it just because the schedule calls for doing something else.

Time Alone, Time Together

If the schedule is posted in the classrooms you visit, you may see terms such as "circle time," "work time," or "choice time." These tell you when children will participate in an activity together as a group, and when they are free to select activities on their own.

Circle time, which shouldn't last more than 10 or 15 minutes, is a time when children learn what it means to be part of a classroom community and develop the skills to participate effectively in a group. During circle time, teachers greet children, talk about the plans for the day, and encourage children to share ideas. Sometimes each teacher takes a small group so children have more opportunities to be active participants.

If your visit coincides with a circle time, you should observe maximum participation by the children and minimum time spent just sitting and listening to the teacher. Circle time activities might include storytelling, finger plays, music and movement activities, exercises, and games. These age-appropriate types of activities take into account children's attention spans, interests, and abilities and create the most successful circle times.

Choice time—also called work time or free play—is when children are free to decide which interest areas they want to play in and what they want to do. They may play alone or with one or two other children, exploring materials and trying out their ideas. However, you may observe very different approaches to choice time in the classrooms you visit, and the differences are significant.

In one program, the children rotate from one activity to another at a signal from the teacher. In the art area, the children paste construction paper flowers in precut flower pots. In the block area, each child is given a set number of blocks with which to build. At the table toy area, the children play a matching game with the teacher. The teacher tells the children when to go on to the next activity.

In another program, the children have real choices to make—first about where to go, and then about what to do when they get there. The dramatic play area is set up as a shoe store with many shoe boxes, the kind of stool the sales clerks use, and foot measuring devices. The art area has playdough, markers, paper, and two easels set up with paints and brushes. The table toy area offers a selection of puzzles and games.

These two situations represent two very different ways for children to spend their time. In the first classroom, despite the appearance of variety, children's choices are restricted and directed by teachers. In the latter example, children take the initiative. Their play time is more likely to be well spent. They learn how to learn because teachers have created an environment rich in opportunities and materials, and encouraged children to make choices and explore.

What are the advantages of encouraging children to make their own choices? By selecting and carrying out their own activities, children learn independence and self-reliance. They also learn to pursue their own ideas. Your child may walk in to school one day and know that she wants to draw a picture of her new puppy. Or she may decide to build a tower to give her doll a view of the classroom. Or he may invite friends to his cave where the bear lives. In their play, children pose questions, ponder solutions, and recall what they have learned from experience. When children have a variety of materials to explore, they practice refining gross and fine motor skills, and develop their imaginations and curiosity.

A Note About Two-Year-Olds

If you are looking at programs for your two-year-old child, you should be concerned about a program that treats twos like preschoolers. As we have stated, a program for twos should be very different from a preschool program. The environment should be less structured and the schedule more flexible. The daily routines of saying hello and good-bye, preparing and eating food, napping, diapering and toileting, and dressing occupy a significant part of a two-year-old's day. Routines are themselves learning opportunities, rather than events to be "gotten through." Some routines (such as dressing and diapering) may require distinct space in the classroom.

In addition to areas set aside for routines, two-year-olds need plenty of space for free play. Like preschoolers, two-year-olds also like to have choices, but they can only handle a limited number of options. Moreover, they do better with fewer planned activities at set times. Teachers then can take their cues from the children, observing how the children explore interesting materials. Because most twos are not yet ready to share toys and equipment, you should see duplicates of popular toys rather than a great variety. Two-year-olds like to stick together. They may not want to break up into different activity groups, but rather all use similar materials at the same time.

What You Should See When You Visit

The environment and daily schedule we have described in this chapter support preschool children's developmental needs and promote positive behavior. Looking around the classroom when you visit will give you lots of clues. Here are some things to look for:

- Clearly defined interest areas, each offering a different kind of activity.

- Materials displayed on low shelves labeled with pictures and words so children can reach what they need and replace items when they are finished.

- A schedule that offers a good balance of active and quiet times, including one or two periods outdoors each day.

- Sufficient time for children to select their own activities and to play uninterrupted for an extended period.

- Children involved in activities and taking responsibility for selecting and returning the materials they use.

What You Should *Not* See

Children's behavior will alert you to examine more closely whether the environment is well designed and the schedule is appropriate. Here are some things that should make you suspicious.

- Children wandering around the room looking for things to do.

- Children required to stand in line and wait for the next activity or routine rather than being meaningfully involved in transitions.

- Teachers not actively interacting with children or extending their play.

- Children running aimlessly during outdoor time because there are no other choices available.

- Teachers telling children to sit still or not touch things.

Questions to Ask

- What kinds of choices can children make during the day?

- How long is your circle time, and what do you do during that period?

- What kinds of activities do you plan for outdoors?

- How does the space encourage children with disabilities or other special concerns to participate?

- Where do children store their private belongings?

– 5 –
Promoting Social and Emotional Skills

To many parents, one of the most attractive aspects of a preschool experience is that children learn to play and get along with others. This is an important plus and an excellent reason for choosing to send a child to preschool. The research we described earlier in this book shows that children who have friends, who know how to work cooperatively with others, and who can manage their emotions are happier and more likely to be successful in school and in life than children who do not have these skills. A child's social experiences during the first five years—at home and in group settings— form the foundation for what we now call "emotional intelligence."

You have been helping your child develop emotional intelligence since birth. Remember that first "social smile" when your baby responded to your smiling, nodding face, and you knew the smile wasn't caused by gas? Not long after that you began mimicking the sounds your baby made and the "conversation" continued back and forth, sound by sound, in a kind of social dance. These early experiences were your child's first lessons in the give and take of social interactions.

You also taught your child about feelings. For example, when a brightly colored ball suddenly rolled into view, your child probably showed great surprise and excitement. In all likelihood, you responded with a similar level of excitement: "Look, a ball!" thus mirroring your child's feelings. Similarly, if your child was frightened or upset, you probably responded with soothing and caring words: "That big noise scared you didn't it? It's okay." By acknowledging your child's feelings, you laid the foundation for empathy—an important component of emotional intelligence.

You were also helping your child develop social and emotional skills when you set clear limits. No one enjoys or wants to play with a child who is a tyrant and always demands his or her own way. So early on, you began guiding your child's behavior, teaching what was acceptable behavior and what was not. Setting limits helped your child to feel safe and learn self-control.

Doesn't it make sense, then, that a major underlying goal of a good preschool program should be to strengthen and enhance your child's social and emotional skills? When you begin looking at preschools, you will see that programs differ in their approaches to building these skills. As an example, here are two situations you might see.

In one classroom, a four-year-old has just been sent by the teacher to sit on the time-out chair after hitting another child who grabbed his truck. You hear the teacher say, "Bobby, you know we don't hit in this room. I want you to sit in the time-out chair until you can remember to use your words and not your fists."

In another program, a teacher is kneeling with her arms around two four-year-olds who are obviously upset. She says in a calm voice, "You are both upset. Tell me one at a time what the problem is." After listening to both children, she restates what she heard and then says, "We need to think of a way you can both have what you want and no one gets hurt. Any ideas?" After making a number of suggestions, the children agree to try out one and report back on what happens.

The idea of time-out is not a bad one; we all need ways to calm down when we are angry and overwhelmed. Unfortunately, too often the "time-out chair" is used as a punishment, and children learn very little from being sent to sit and "think." A more successful approach is to teach children how to solve problems themselves by letting them know their concerns have been heard and helping them generate solutions to their problem. If we want children to grow up to be caring and responsible individuals who can resolve conflicts when they come up, their preschool experiences should promote these values and abilities.

Social and Emotional Skills—What's Involved

When we speak of social skills and emotional skills, we are also addressing discipline—a topic of great interest to all parents and to teachers. All children need discipline, but what is the goal? We believe the goal is to help children develop self-discipline, the ability to control their own behavior and act responsibly, showing respect for oneself and others. Children develop self-discipline when adults have realistic expectations, set clear limits, and build positive relationships with each child.

Social and emotional skills, including self-discipline, are not something we can "give" to children or teach in a lesson. They are attributes and a sense of self that are cultivated and nurtured through ongoing interactions children have every day with caring adults and other children. We see evidence that these skills are emerging when children show a growing confidence in their abilities, develop increasing self-control, and are able to develop and maintain friendships with other children, including children who are different from them.

Growing self-confidence. During the preschool years, children are developing a sense of who they are and what they can do. Confident children believe that they will succeed at whatever they do and that they can ask adults for help. Such children are curious and eager to find out about things. They pose interesting questions ("What foods does our guinea pig like best?" or "Where do shadows come from?") and respond positively when adults encourage them to seek answers to the things that interest and intrigue them.

Sometimes preschool children are overconfident, often misjudging their capabilities. At the same time, they can easily become frustrated and discouraged if they regularly fail at tasks they are expected to do. For these reasons, teachers must have realistic expectations of what children can do so they can plan experiences that are sufficiently challenging but also attainable. Skilled teachers take an interest in what children are interested in—whether it's watching where ants go with their bread crumbs or figuring out how to make pink paint—and encourage children to experiment and find answers to their own questions. They are good observers who know when to step in and help a child who is frustrated and when to hold back and allow a child to solve a problem independently.

Developing self-control. Children with self-control are learning how to manage their emotions and control their actions in age-appropriate ways. Preschool children have strong feelings and often lack the verbal skills needed to express them, so they may lash out physically toward others. Preschool children also typically have a range of fears—about monsters, being injured or kidnapped, and losing a loved one. To help children develop self-control, skilled teachers create a sense of safety in the classroom and provide many opportunities for children to play out their fears in constructive ways—through play, creative art, and a well-balanced day of active and quiet activities. They teach children to use words to communicate their needs ("I don't like it when you hit me. Stop it!") and help them learn alternative ways to resolve conflicts.

Making friends. Children who have friends usually like to go to school. They know how to approach other children, contribute to a discussion, show appreciation for another child's work, and take turns. They might, for example, watch two children playing grocery store before making a suggestion that leads to inclusion: "I'm a truck driver, and I have some food to deliver. Where should I put it?" They usually have good communication skills and are capable of exchanging ideas, feelings, and concepts with others. And they are cooperative—able to balance their own needs with those of others in the group. In preschool, and for the rest of their lives, children will be with people who are different from them in a variety of ways. In our increasingly diverse world, it is essential for children to develop an appreciation and respect for all people. These attitudes have to be nurtured over time by caring adults who understand and value their importance.

What Happens in Preschool

Unfortunately, not all preschools pay adequate attention to cultivating children's social skills and emotional well-being. Indeed, some are so focused on "preparing children for school"—for example, teaching colors, numbers, letters, and facts—they forget the most important lesson of all: that social and emotional development form the foundation for school success. For this reason, it's important to know what you should expect from high-quality preschool programs.

Children feel the classroom belongs to them. A preschool, like a family, is a community with its own distinct values and traditions. One way to build a community is to have photographs of children's families displayed throughout the classroom. Check the books and pictures in the room; they should reflect the children themselves as well as people of different cultures and different abilities. Materials should show people of different races, sexes, and ages in a variety of ways that are free of stereotyping. Look for walls that are decorated with children's work rather than commercial posters or artwork that all looks the same. Because children learn to read their own names before they learn to read other words, you should see children's names in several places—on cubbies, artwork, mail boxes, and on a sign-in sheet. To convey the idea that everyone has a role in taking care of the classroom, look for a job chart.

You can also look for evidence of a few rules. Clear and consistent limits make children feel safe. When children help create the rules for their classroom, they are more likely to follow them. Here are some examples:

- Use words instead of hitting.

- Walk in the classroom.

- Put everything back where it belongs.

- We help each other.

Children have opportunities to participate in a group and to play with others. There should be a balance throughout the day of times to play with one or two others and for group experiences. Circle time offers children a chance to learn how to participate in a group and to promote a sense of community in the classroom. Sitting in a circle conveys two important ideas: that everyone is an equally important member of the classroom community and that we all want to see and hear one another.

Circle time often begins with everyone singing together. Then there is time for sharing and discussing topics that are of interest to the children. The teacher may introduce a new activity or new materials that the children can use. Other opportunities to gather as a group may be to listen to a story or participate in a small group activity. At the end of the day, many teachers gather the children together to review what took place and talk about plans for the following day. Each of these group times provides children with opportunities to practice listening and speaking skills and to experience belonging to a community of learners.

The daily schedule should include ample time periods (at least an hour each morning and each afternoon in a full-day program) when children can select their own activities. Children become self-directed learners when they are encouraged to explore and discover on their own and with others. When children play together on an activity of their choice, they share their knowledge, solve problems together, and develop social skills. Here's an example of what might occur:

> *Shontelle and Amy decide they want to build a maze for Skippy, the classroom guinea pig. At the teacher's suggestion, they first draw a picture of the maze they want to make. Selecting unit blocks, they begin work. "Look," says Amy, "You're not following the picture. That block needs to go this way." Several animated discussions take place as the two girls build their maze. When they are almost finished, Billy enters the block area and says, "Wow! That's neat. Should I get Skippy so you can try out your maze?" The two builders agree, and Billy then joins the building crew. Pretty soon, other children come over to watch and comment on how Skippy is navigating the maze.*

When children are able to select their own play activities, they often come up with creative ideas, try them out, and see what effect they can have on their environment. These experiences are also the most effective way for children to acquire and strengthen social skills.

Children need to be taught a system for resolving conflicts. Conflicts are part of life, and they occur in every classroom. One of the most common conflicts among preschool children concerns sharing. While we certainly agree that the ability to share is important, it is not always possible for young children. Telling children they have to share is not sufficient. For younger preschoolers especially, teachers should provide duplicates of materials they know will be very popular. Eventually, teachers and children together can establish systems for taking turns.

Even with these steps, conflicts will emerge in the classroom, just as they do at home. It would be relatively quick and simple for adults to solve these conflicts for children, but skilled teachers and parents use conflicts as opportunities to teach children how to solve problems peacefully. Because conflicts often generate strong feelings, it's best to begin by giving children strategies for calming down: counting to ten, taking deep breaths, going to a "calm down" place in the classroom to relax on some soft pillows. Here's how a teacher might lead children to a solution by going through a series of specific steps. (You can teach your child to resolve conflicts by following the same steps at home).

- ***Defining the problem:*** Putting an arm around each child, a teacher bends down and says, "I see we have a problem here. Tell me about it." Each child gives his or her view of what happened. The teacher then restates what she hears to verify the facts with the children.

- ***Generating solutions:*** The next step is to come up with some possible solutions. "Can you think of some ways you each could use the truck? I'll write down your ideas, and then you can decide which one you want to try first."

- ***Agreeing on a solution and trying it out:*** The last step is to agree on which solution to try and let the children know they can come back and reevaluate if that solution doesn't work. "OK, so here's what you want to try. You're going to build a garage together, and one will drive the truck, the other will be the repair person to fix the truck. Then you'll switch roles. I think that's a good solution. Try it out. If it doesn't work, come back and we can try another idea."

In classrooms where these steps are taught, children eventually begin resolving conflicts without the teacher's help. Teaching children to resolve conflicts is not only important for their social development, but it promotes cognitive skills as well. Additionally, it leads to a peaceful classroom environment, which is conducive to emotional well-being and learning.

What You Should See When You Visit

The best way to assess the emotional climate of a classroom is to spend an hour or more as a visitor. Notice what materials teachers have selected for different interest areas. Pay special attention to how teachers interact with children to promote the development of social and emotional skills.

The Environment

Here are just a few examples of what you might see in different interest areas.

- **House corner:** Props that represent different cultural groups, dress-up clothes that inspire children to reenact previous experiences.

- **Table toy area:** Duplicates of favorite toys to minimize the demands for sharing, a sand timer or waiting list so children know when their turn comes.

- **Cooking:** A class cookbook of recipes the children have tried, with photographs of the cooks and illustrations by the children.

- **Library area:** Books featuring people of different cultures, different kinds of families, people with disabilities, and stories on topics such as friendships, helping others, handling conflicts, and dealing with fears.

- **Art area:** Paints and crayons in a variety of skin tones.

The Teachers

The most important indicator of a positive social climate is how teachers interact with children. When you visit, look and listen from the perspective of your child. It's a good sign if you see and hear teachers doing the following:

- Bending down to talk with a child: "Let me listen very carefully so I know what is bothering you."

- Helping children to appreciate each other's strengths and interests: "I bet Tyrone can help you with that puzzle. You know how he likes puzzles," or, "Be sure to show your book about cats to Jenny. Remember she told us about her new kitten?"

- Accepting mistakes as part of the learning process: "Whoops, that didn't work. Let's get a sponge and mop it up and think of another way to get the water out of the water table."

- Describing the behavior they want to see in positive terms: "Keep the water inside the water table. The floor gets slippery if it's wet."

- Encouraging children to help one another: "Jamal, I think if you ask Lee Ming, he will help you to carry the sawhorse outside."

- Demonstrating good manners: "Thank you for holding the door for me. That was very helpful because my hands were full."

- Interpreting feelings so children learn to recognize how others feel: "Look at Andre's face. Can you see how upset he is? Let's see what we can do to help."

- Welcoming families to visit at any time and encouraging them to participate and contribute to the program.

What You Should *Not* See

- Teachers focusing on children's misbehavior without dealing with the problems that cause it.

- Children being sent to a time-out chair to sit and "think" about what they did wrong.

- Teachers talking down to children or shouting at them from across the room.

- Teachers setting standards for behavior that are not appropriate for children, for example, having children sit quietly or wait in line for long periods.

Questions to Ask

- What are your most important goals for children who attend this preschool?

- How do you help children learn to get along with others?

- How do you help a child who is very shy or timid?

- How do you handle a child who is very aggressive?

- What rules do you have for your classroom and how do children learn about them?

- For what reasons would a child be disciplined and how?

- How do you help children learn to solve conflicts when they come up?

What Happens at Home

There are many ways you nurture your child's social and emotional skills at home.

WHEN YOUR CHILD...	YOU MIGHT SAY...	THIS HELPS YOUR CHILD...
Screams with frustration because she can't get the pieces to fit in a new puzzle	*"This is a hard puzzle isn't it? Let's look carefully at each piece and see if that helps us figure out where it goes."*	Develop self-confidence and learn to persist even when tasks are difficult
Throws sand towards another child playing in a sand box	*"Sand is not for throwing. It hurts to get sand in your eyes. You can scoop the sand and dig in it."*	Develop self-control. It teaches him what he can do as well as what is not acceptable and why
Falls apart at the end of the day	*"It looks like we both need some quiet time to relax. How about reading a book together before we make dinner?"*	Understand her own feelings and that adults will be there to help
Has a friend over to play but they seem at a loss about what to do	*"Let's make a list of all the things you can do together. Then you can decide what you want to do first. I'll help you get started if you want."*	Have positive experiences with friends by expanding the possibilities for playing together in constructive ways

– 6 –

Strengthening Physical Skills

Taking children's physical development for granted is easy because you may not have had to do very much to encourage your child to sit alone, stand, crawl, and walk. Quite naturally, your child may have developed the fine muscle skills to hold a cup, place shapes in matching holes, and turn the pages of a book. Yet you played an important role, providing appropriate materials and equipment, allocating time for your child to practice new skills, and serving as a cheerleader. You intuitively knew that physical fitness was central to your child's well-being and ability to learn. In preschool, you want the teachers to plan increasingly challenging experiences to build and expand the physical skills your child will need, not only for many different sports, but also for reading, writing, and working with different kinds of equipment and materials.

When you visit preschools, you may find vastly different approaches to promoting children's physical skills. Here's what you might see.

In one program, the children are playing a game of Duck-Duck-Goose. They sit in a circle while one child moves around the outside. She taps a child on the shoulder, and that child chases her around the circle until she returns to where he was sitting and sits there. The game continues until all the children have had a turn. During outdoor time, the children run around the yard and take turns on swings and climbers as the teachers chat with each other and keep an eye on the children.

At a second program, the children are moving their bodies in a variety of ways to show how spiders would walk across a hot roof. During outdoor time, they choose from a variety of activities: drawing on the pavement with colored chalk, walking on balance beams, throwing balls against a wall and catching them, painting with large brushes and water on the wood fence. One teacher brings a child in a wheelchair over to a group throwing balls against the wall and hands her a ball to throw and catch. Another teacher stands by the climber in case anyone needs help.

In the first example, the children are playing a game that requires them to spend most of their time waiting for a turn to run around the circle. Outdoors, the teachers use their time to socialize as they watch children. In contrast, the second program asks children to think creatively about how to use their bodies as they move. Teachers encourage and guide children's play outdoors, just as they do in the classroom.

Physical Skills—What's Involved

The benefits of promoting physical skills are well documented. The Surgeon General's Report on Physical Activity and Well-Being (1996) states that physical activity contributes significantly to personal health and well-being. California's Position Statement on Physical Fitness (1995), which has been endorsed by over fifty organizations, highlights the contributions of physical education in the early grades to children's academic achievement, general health, self-esteem, stress management, and social development. And we know from brain research that movement literally "wakes up" the brain. Quality preschools, therefore, encourage children by providing them with opportunities to move skillfully, manipulate objects, balance and control the body, and refine fine muscle skills.

Moving skillfully. The physical skills children master during the preschool years are ones that most children tackle enthusiastically: running, leaping, jumping, skipping, climbing, hopping, moving to music, and moving under, around, and over objects. With practice and guidance, children gain coordination and become increasingly agile at each of these maneuvers. They learn, for example, how to transfer hand positions as they climb, to jump from platforms and roll, to skip alternating their feet, and to make their movements match the beat of a march.

Manipulating objects. Young children are drawn to objects. They can hardly resist the urge to touch, throw, catch, kick, strike, and move objects from place to place. The skills involved in manipulating objects are ones children will need for more advanced learning and specialized sports. Therefore, in preschool, children need access to a variety of objects and places to move them.

Balancing and controlling the body. Children learn to balance and control the weight of their bodies. This process begins when babies gain the control to hold up their heads and it continues in a natural progression as they learn to sit, crawl, stand, and take their first steps. In the preschool years, children learn to reach, twist, turn, bend, stretch, lift, carry, push and pull, and walk across a balance beam. They love challenges that allow them to use these skills such as finding a way to move across the floor using only one foot and two hands or hanging from a bar by their knees.

Refining fine muscle skills. In preschool, children's fine muscle skills are just beginning to develop. Most do not have the hand and wrist control or refined eye-hand coordination needed to complete tasks such as writing or copying letters off a blackboard. In fact, asking children to perform these tasks may cause frustration and discouragement. Preschoolers need many opportunities to develop strength in their fine muscles so they can tie shoes, draw, cut with scissors, balance blocks, and complete other appropriate tasks.

What Happens in Preschool

As children work to master basic physical skills, they need plenty of time for indoor and outdoor physical play. Two- and three-year-olds are still quite uncoordinated but are eager to try their skills at throwing and catching, kicking and jumping. They need plenty of time for indoor and outdoor physical play. Four- and five-year-olds are gaining greater control over their movements and are becoming more coordinated. All preschoolers expand their repertoire of skills when they have opportunities to use appropriate materials, play experiences that provide practice in specific skills, and when they are encouraged by adults to take appropriate risks.

Too many preschools and elementary schools take the development of physical skills, especially large motor skills, for granted. Free play, although good, is not enough. Children also need planned experiences and specific guidance to develop large and small motor skills.

Children need several periods of the day when they can be physically active, indoors and outside. When you visit, note whether the daily schedule provides ample time each day for children to be outdoors (thirty to sixty minutes at least each morning and afternoon). Look to see whether there is an indoor choice time (an hour in the morning and again in the afternoon if it is a full-day program) when children can explore, move, and act on objects. Observe what children

do during these periods of the day and how teachers encourage them to participate in activities or use equipment. For example, you may see a teacher set hoops and suggest a game where children jump from one hoop to another. Or, you might see a teacher making suggestions to a child who is having trouble climbing on a jungle gym.

Children need materials and equipment that promote large and small muscle skills. Appropriate equipment and materials—indoors as well as outdoors—inspire children to exercise their large muscles. Large hollow building blocks, clay to pound, a workbench with real tools and wood, and ample space for movement activities all promote large muscle skills. For developing small muscle skills, children need materials for drawing, gluing, and cutting; toys that interlock and fit together; and objects to sort and order. For a child with a physical disability, you'll want to see appropriate accommodations, such as equipment that is wheelchair accessible, modifications to materials (such as pegs on puzzle pieces) that make them easy to grasp, and computer programs that enable a child with limited hand control to draw and manipulate objects on the screen. (see appendix B)

Children need opportunities to express themselves freely through movement. Most young children can communicate more easily physically than verbally. For example, with a bit of adult encouragement, they can act out ideas from a story, pretend to be an animal or the wind, and show how a flower grows from a seed. Music periods provide many opportunities for children to express themselves through movement. For example, you might see a group of children moving their bodies as they listen to different kinds of music.

What You Should See When You Visit

Spend some time observing children indoors and outdoors when you visit preschool programs. The equipment and materials will tell you a lot about how the program strengthens children's physical skills. Note also what teachers do to encourage children.

The Environment

Here are just a few examples of the kinds of equipment and materials to look for outdoors and in classroom interest areas.

- **Outdoors:** Sturdy climbing equipment and swings with cushioning materials underneath; tricycles and riding toys; plastic or foam bats and balls; rubber balls of all sizes; hoops; balance beams; a sand box that can be covered when not in use and toys for scooping, pouring and digging; perhaps a work bench with tools.

- **House corner:** Dress-up clothes that require zipping, buckling, snapping, or buttoning; dolls and accessories; dishes and utensils.

- **Table toys:** Pegs and peg boards, puzzles, interlocking construction toys, pattern blocks, beads and laces, self-help skills boards, small objects to sort.

- **Cooking:** Utensils for mixing, beating, shaking, measuring, scraping, cutting, flipping, and pouring; mixing bowls.

- **Art area:** Crayons, markers, pencils, plenty of plain drawing paper, blunt scissors, clay, and playdough.

- **Blocks:** Blocks organized by size and shape; block accessories such as cars, people figures, animals, colored cubes; ample room to build.

The Teachers

Teachers play a crucial role in encouraging children to try out new physical skills and refine and practice ones they have mastered. Look at what they do. For example, you'll want to see teachers who:

- Encourage children to use different physical skills such as hopping, skipping, jumping, throwing and catching, striking, balancing.

- Invite children to use their bodies to explore the concept of speed: "Everyone find a space where you have room to move. First we are going to move slowly. Can you show me how a turtle would move? A worm? A leaf falling gently from a tree?"

- Provide specific instruction on a new skill: "Galloping like a horse is kind of tricky. Watch my feet and I'll do it slowly so you can try it one step at a time."

- Reassure a child who is taking a risk: "The top of the slide is pretty high. I'll stand here until you feel comfortable."

- Encourage a child: "If you hold the paper in your hand this way, it might be easier to cut it with the scissors."

What You Should *Not* See

- Children sitting for long periods of time watching and listening.

- Children doing fine motor tasks that are too difficult and frustrating.

- Teachers using outdoor time as their break rather than playing with the children and organizing activities.

Questions to Ask

- How much time do the children spend outdoors each day?

- What activities do you plan for them outdoors?

- What kinds of large motor skills do you hope children will master in preschool?

- How do you help children practice and refine small muscle skills?

What Happens at Home

There are many ways you promote your child's physical skills at home.

WHEN YOU AND YOUR CHILD...	YOU MIGHT SAY...	THIS HELPS YOUR CHILD...
Go on a walk	*"Let's think of all the ways we can get from here to the house."*	Think creatively and move in a variety of ways
Play a game batting a balloon around and keeping it in the air	*"Let's try hitting the balloon with different parts of our bodies."*	Coordinate movements and solve a problem
Run together until both of you are out of breath	*"Put your hand on your heart. Can you feel it beating? It's thanking you for giving it exercise."*	Develop body awareness and an appreciation of good health habits

– 7 –
Exploring Reading and Writing

Literacy begins at birth. The early reading and writing experiences children have help prepare them for later success in school. That's why rich and varied language and literacy experiences at home and at preschool are so important. Children who have been read to, who know nursery rhymes and chants, who hear a great deal of language, and who are familiar with many words are at a tremendous advantage. When it comes to learning to read and write, children must be familiar with language and use it to communicate ideas, desires, and feelings with other people. Literacy skills include listening, comprehending, speaking, reading, and writing.

Think about how your child's literacy skills have been developing since birth. As an infant, he or she responded to the rhythm, patterns, and the tone of your voice as well as those of the other adults around. By the end of the first year, your baby communicated intentionally—making sounds while pointing at a desired object or while raising his or her arms to be carried. Your child's brain was "wired" for language development every time you sang or read a story. Now, approaching age three, your child is communicating with words and increasing in vocabulary daily. You want to choose a preschool that will continue to enhance these skills.

When you look at preschools for your child, you are likely to notice differences in the kind of language and literacy experiences they offer children.

One program sets aside time each day for children to sit quietly at tables and do reading and writing worksheets. The teachers say it's important for children to learn to sit still, follow directions, and practice the skills they will need for reading and writing later on.

At another program, children do their own writing or the teacher writes down children's stories. There are writing materials in many parts of the room and child-made signs are evident. Children don't have workbooks, but the director points out samples of children's writing the classroom: signs on block structures, a sign-in list where children have written their names, and pictures the children have drawn.

These two programs reflect different beliefs about how children explore reading and writing. The first program asks children to work on skills by doing drill and practice exercises. While children may learn to complete worksheets successfully, this approach does little to interest children in reading and writing. Such exercises do not connect what children see and touch in the real world with reading and writing. The second program, where children are engaged in real writing activities, is more appropriate. Reading and writing experiences in preschool (as in all grades) should enable children to feel competent and increase their desire to learn more.

What's Involved in Reading and Writing

Research on literacy development in recent years emphasizes that many different kinds of early literacy experiences in preschool help children become successful readers and writers later on. Quality preschool programs focus on developing skills in three areas.

Listening and speaking. The preschool years are a time of enormous vocabulary development. As children play with one another, they should be encouraged to use language to communicate ideas and feelings, to ask and answer questions, and to tell stories about events that happened to them. Teachers and other adults can model and teach conversational skills. They can encourage children to think about the meaning of words, to manipulate sounds in words (rhymes), and to pay attention to stories and talk about them. An important way that children learn is by connecting what they hear to their own experiences. Therefore, storytelling should involve children in thinking about how the story relates to their lives.

Early reading. Reading is about getting meaning from print. Readers know that written words convey messages. Because reading involves making connections between words and ideas, children benefit from opportunities to hear new vocabulary, talk about the meaning of words, and connect words with images. Young children need to explore books—to be read to and to read the same books over and over again. They gradually recognize that stories have a beginning, middle, and end, and they are eager to tell you the story. When children realize that words are symbols for ideas and thoughts, they have made a great leap in literacy development. Over time, children realize that printed letters represent specific words.

Early writing. Learning to read goes hand-in-hand with learning to write. To become writers, children have to learn that writing involves using symbols for speech and putting these symbols on paper. They learn when they see adults writing for a variety of purposes and when they themselves have a reason to communicate their own ideas on paper. In the beginning, children use picture writing and scribble writing to communicate on paper. When they discover that their writing is appreciated and encouraged, they move on to stringing random letters together. As they learn to connect the sounds of language with the letter symbols, they use beginning consonants to represent words.

What Happens in Preschool

Whatever their age and experience, all children bring to preschool a variety of experiences with print. Some children will read their own names or recognize street signs, the M for McDonald's, or certain food containers. Your child's reading- and writing-related experiences in preschool should build from this natural base, using what he or she already knows and adding on from there. There are several kinds of experiences that are essential.

Children are read to every day. Children who have enjoyable experiences with stories and poetry want to be readers themselves. You will want to see a preschool classroom that includes a variety of picture books and poetry that reflects the cultural backgrounds of the

children and are relevant to their experiences. By using books children enjoy, teachers can build children's excitement about reading.

Children learn in a print-rich environment. Signs and labels should be visible at children's eye level throughout the room. Look for children's names prominently displayed in the classroom and used for a purpose—to label cubbies, identify belongings and work, identify jobs for each day, and so on. The alphabet should be displayed at children's eye level and in a place where they will refer to it, such as a library or art area. This allows children to use the alphabet as a reference to make connections between the words they know and the letters and sounds of the alphabet.

Children need opportunities and reasons to write every day. Note whether there is an attractive writing center and a variety of writing tools as well as rubber and magnetic letters that appeal to children. Writing is important because it's a way to share information. Children learn reasons for writing when they sign their names for attendance (with a scribble, a letter or two, or a complete name), draw picture stories and then "tell" the story, make signs, write messages, write thank-you letters, and make lists.

What You Should See When You Visit

When you visit you want to look for evidence that reading and writing are a part of many daily activities. That way children can make discoveries about letters, the sounds and symbols of language, and the purposes of writing all day long in everything they do.

The Environment

At the most basic, notice whether there is print around the room. Are children's names used to label a storage cabinet or shelf? Are books, writing tools, and paper in use? Look for signs that show that play in the interest areas of the classroom promotes reading and writing. Here are some examples:

- **Block area:** A basket containing markers, index cards or poster board, and masking tape, so children can make signs for their block buildings; books with buildings, bridges, tools, and construction sites so that children learn they can get ideas from books; toy traffic signs.

- **House corner:** Magazines, cookbooks, telephone books, paper, and pencils for children to use in their pretend play; food containers for a grocery store; newspapers; restaurant menus; story books children can read to their "babies."

- **Cooking:** Illustrated and written recipes that children can refer to as they cook so they know that writing serves a purpose.

- **Music and movement:** Chart paper with songs and rhymes children are learning.

- **Library area:** Soft pillows and chairs where children can curl up with a book; a rich variety of picture books and story tapes; writing materials; paper; the alphabet displayed at children's eye level.

- **Computer area:** Picture and word directions for children to follow; several reading- and writing-related programs that hold their interest and can be used independently.

- **Art area:** Markers, crayons; paper for drawing and writing; playdough and clay to develop small muscle control.

The Teachers

In addition to what you can see in interest areas, interactions between teachers and children also promote literacy development. Children learn that print is an important means of communication when the following activities are part of their classroom experiences:

- making shopping lists for classroom and cooking supplies

- dictating ideas in a discussion that the teacher records on a chart

- writing thank-you notes to classroom visitors or people visited on a trip

- noticing street signs on a walk

- saying words said out loud as they are written on a chart

- seeing someone point to the words on a page as a story is read aloud

- encouraging message writing and sign-in sheets

An important part of helping children grow as readers and writers is encouraging talking. Listen for a classroom where conversations are promoted by adults who listen carefully to what children say and do and make comments and ask the kinds of questions that help children to think and explain. For example:

- Asking questions about a book: "Why do you think the little girl is sad?" "What do you think will happen next?" "What would you do if you were Arthur?" "Have you ever felt like Francine?"

- Talking about children's work: "How did you make that new color?" "How is this collage different from the first one you made?" "What happened when you added sand to the paint?" "Let's make a sign for your block structure so no one will move it."

- Making children aware of sounds and how they use their bodies: "How does it sound?" "How would you make the drum sound soft?" "What would happen if…?"

- Helping children become better listeners: "If we look at the person who is talking, he'll know we're listening."

- Using children's names in a variety of ways: "Let's start a waiting list for the computer area so everyone knows who is waiting for a turn."

When listening, speaking, reading, and writing activities are infused throughout the day, children can learn at their own pace in appropriate ways as they play. Learning to read and write is not a race. Some children learn to read in preschool and kindergarten. Others may not read until well into second or third grade. But even though different children are ready to read and write at different ages, all children benefit from rich literacy experiences.

What You Should *Not* See

- Children required to sit and do paper and pencil activities such as copying the alphabet or completing ditto sheets and workbooks about letters and sounds.

- Teachers working with children in formal reading groups.

- Teachers talking to children primarily by asking factual questions that require one word or simple straightforward answers.

Questions to Ask

- How often do you read to children?

- What kinds of books or poems do you find children like best?

- What do the children talk about at circle time?

- In what ways do you help children learn about reading and writing?

- How do you keep track of each child's early reading and writing skills?

- What do you suggest parents do at home?

What Happens at Home

You can promote your child's emerging language, reading, and writing skills in many of the daily or weekly activities you do together.

WHEN YOU AND YOUR CHILD...	YOU MIGHT SAY...	THIS HELPS YOUR CHILD LEARN TO...
Read library books together	*"Who is this story about?"* *"What happened?"* *"How did he feel?"* *"Now you tell me the story."*	Listen to a story and explain what happened Use language to describe events and express feelings
Look at family photos together	*"Who's that, and what is he doing?* *Do you remember what happened that day?"*	Use language to describe events Interpret pictures Recall a story about an event
Make a grocery list	*"Let's think about what we need and write it on this list."*	Write for a purpose Learn vocabulary
Talk about the signs that you see around you	*"That red sign says STOP, so I'm going to stop the car and look around before starting again."*	Recognize words on signs
Write a story together	*"You tell me a story and I'll write it down. Then you can draw pictures to go with it."*	Use language to express ideas Recognize that stories have a beginning, middle, and end

– 8 –
Discovering Mathematical Relationships

Mathematics is about organizing information, comparing quantities, and seeing relationships. Learning the concepts and language of mathematics—more, less, equal, a fraction of, multiples of, and so on—helps children to make sense of the world as they find order in patterns, make predictions, and solve problems.

Much of what you have already done with your child has set the stage for discovering mathematical relationships. For example, the routines you established related to sleeping, eating, and cuddling are the beginning of logical patterns that your child probably has come to expect because they happen almost every day. You may also see evidence that your child is beginning to think mathematically. You may have heard your child say: "My doll is bigger than yours." "He has more candy than I do." Preschoolers make comparisons all the time—they want to jump higher, run faster, and stay awake longer. When you say, "I'll be off the phone in a minute" or "Let's put all your toy cars in one container," you are building the language of mathematics into your child's brain and making connections between math and everyday life.

Preschool programs may view mathematical learning opportunities differently.

At one preschool, the children recite numbers from memory each morning and are expected to write answers to addition problems. Children who can not yet write numbers use crayons to color number symbols.

At another preschool, the director says that it is important for children to hold real objects as they count. The children spend time grouping like objects and comparing objects. In one class, the children have their shoes off and are putting them into piles. The teacher says they will be making a graph to show how many have shoes with laces, buckles, Velcro, etc.

The second program recognizes that children need concrete experiences to acquire a sense of numbers; the other does not. Just as reading is not simply recognizing letters and sounds, mathematics is not simply recognizing numerals. When we teach children to memorize math facts, they learn the facts but may be unable to apply them to solve problems. The preschool years are the time to build on children's concrete interest in math by using real materials and encouraging them to solve real problems.

What's Involved in Math

You may remember learning math by memorizing rules, using flashcards, and reciting math facts. Given our technological age and the role of computers and calculators, today's children need more than facts. They need to be able to notice patterns; collect information; organize, interpret, and explain data; and communicate findings. Certainly they will have to find answers, but first they will need to reason and solve problems. These skills can be strengthened in preschool as children explore many aspects of mathematical thinking while they play.

Patterns and relationships. Patterns and relationships are essential to understanding our number system, ordering information, and solving problems. In preschool, children should have many opportunities to sort and classify objects; to study characteristics such as shape, size, and color; to recognize, create, and copy patterns; and to begin to use language to describe and compare relationships. As

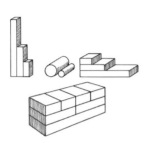

they use materials and words in these ways, they build important mathematical thinking skills.

Number concepts and operations. When preschool children understand number concepts, they know that 3 stands for three objects; that when counting objects, each one is given a number; and that the last number counted in a group tells the quantity of the objects. When preschool children understand what happens as a result of joining, removing, and comparing quantities, they are able to use the basic procedures of addition and subtraction to solve problems.

Estimation. Estimating is about knowing when and how to make a sensible guess to answer a mathematical question. Children in preschool learn to estimate when they predict how many blocks they will need to connect the two buildings or how many cups of sand will fill the bucket.

Geometry and spatial relationships. Young children spend a great deal of time noticing and comparing two- and three-dimensional objects. As they make shapes with playdough, manipulate three-dimensional shapes, put puzzles together, and build with blocks, they explore geometry and spatial relationships. Experiences with building things enable preschool children to explore the properties of different shapes.

Measurement. Preschool children develop an understanding of measurement when they use materials in hands-on activities to explore length and area, time, temperature, mass, and capacity. They make their own measuring tools, such as strings and blocks, and use simple clocks, sand timers, scales, thermometers, measuring cups, and rulers in their explorations.

Probability and statistics. Preschool children learn about probability and statistics when they try to determine whether something is likely to happen and why. Working with data, thinking about predictions, and asking new questions are all essential critical thinking skills that relate to probability. As they toss coins, roll dice, spin spinners, and spill painted beans, they can also learn to describe, question, and discuss what they are doing. Graphs teach them about organizing information.

OUR LEAVES					
				🍀	
				🌿	
				🍂	
		🌿		🍁	
	🍃	🍃		🌸	
🍁	🍃	🍃	🍂	🍁	🌾
🍁	🍃	🍃	🍂	🍂	🍁
MAPLE	ELM	DOG-WOOD	BIRCH	OAK	PINE

What Happens in Preschool

Just as children come to preschool knowing something about language and print, they also come knowing something about math. Some children will be able to count to five, ten, or even twenty. Others will demonstrate an understanding that five objects are more than four. But even when children seem to have an awareness of numbers, they are easily misled by how things look. Five large objects may appear to be more than eight tiny objects. Therefore, in preschool, children should be playing with concrete objects as they learn about mathematical relationships. Here are the kinds of experiences children need.

Children participate in mathematical conversations every day. Much math learning occurs as teachers interact with children. For example, when teachers talk with younger preschoolers about where they are going—under, over, up, on top, through—children learn math. They learn about patterns as they play finger games, recite rhymes or songs, and discuss the daily schedule. Older preschoolers playing with water and sand can experiment with and talk about measurement. When adults comment on what they see in children's work ("You put the same number of circles on the top and the bottom of your picture."), children learn new ways to think about and describe what they have done and better understand their experiences.

Children use concrete or manipulative materials in their explorations. For children to engage in the kinds of explorations required to answer questions and solve problems, they need materials—and lots of them. Objects children can use to sort and classify, build, count and measure, and create designs and patterns are available in many areas of the room so that wherever children play, they can learn about mathematical relationships. There are books about numbers and patterns in the reading area and books about shapes in the block area. Like the alphabet, number symbols and pictorial explanations are accessible to children.

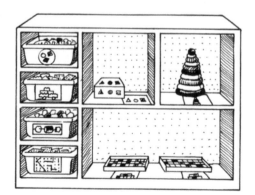

Children solve real mathematical problems every day. Problems that require mathematical thinking come up naturally each day. Whether the problems involve figuring out how to divide a snack, following a recipe, or guessing how many children can fit in a particular space or about how many songs can be sung before lunch, children can be encouraged to participate in solving them. Mathematical thinking is an important part of their daily lives, and they become aware that math serves a real purpose.

What You Should See When You Visit

Children develop mathematical skills and discover mathematical relationships as they play with many different kinds of materials and have conversations about what they are doing. Look at what is in each interest area for children to use and listen to what children talk about with one another and with teachers.

The Environment

Here are some examples of what you might see in different interest areas:

- **Block area:** Blocks organized by shape on the shelves, with labels for each shape and for props.

- **House corner:** Dress-up clothes, props, pots and pans, and cooking utensils on shelves or hung with picture labels, so children can sort and put things away systematically; sufficient forks, knives, spoons, and plates for setting the table.

- **Table toys:** Games, manipulatives, puzzles, and collectibles that children can use to count, sort, build, or otherwise organize at a table or on the floor.

- **Cooking activities:** Measuring spoons, cups, and bowls to use in preparing food.

- **Library:** Books about numbers and shapes.

- **Art area:** Materials to make designs with different shapes, colors, and objects.

- **Sand and water tables:** Different-sized containers and measuring tools.

- **Computers:** Software that stimulates children to explore making shapes of different sizes, create designs, and repeat designs made first with real materials (mirroring).

In addition to what you see in interest areas, many daily classroom activities can have a math focus. You might notice children using mathematical thinking in these ways:

- taking the attendance for the day and thinking about who is here and who is absent

- figuring out how many cups, spoons, or napkins are needed at snack time

- matching shapes as they put objects away, or grouping like things together during clean-up

- taking a survey of favorite lunch foods and making a graph to compare the results

- noticing shapes and patterns on a walk

The Teachers

Listen too for mathematical conversations. Are the teachers using opportunities to engage children in mathematical thinking as they play? For example, do teachers:

- Encourage children to think about their constructions: "Which is taller, shorter, longer…?" "What shapes do you see?" "Which is first, second, third, last?"

- Help children notice designs: "I see you've used red and blue cubes. How do you know which comes next?"

- Encourage logical thinking skills: "How did you decide to put these objects together?" "What are some ways they are alike?" "Where should this one go?"

With this kind of attention to mathematical thinking, children can make progress as they play with a variety of materials.

What You Should *Not* See

- Children working on pencil and paper activities such as coloring a worksheet page, or completing a page of math facts.

- Children drilling with flash cards or reciting number facts.

- A lack of attention to categorizing supplies.

Questions to Ask

- What kinds of materials do children use to sort and build?

- In what ways do you help children to explore patterns?

- How and when do children make estimates?

- What are some favorite books that emphasize mathematical thinking?

- How do you keep track of each child's development of mathematical skills?

- What do you suggest parents do at home?

What Happens at Home

There are many ways you can encourage your child at home to further develop mathematical thinking.

WHEN YOU AND YOUR CHILD...	YOU MIGHT SAY...	THIS HELPS YOUR CHILD LEARN TO...
Set the table	*"How many people are eating dinner tonight?* *How many plates do we need?* *How many forks? Let's count them out—one fork for Mom, one for Steve..."*	Match one-to-one when counting. Count objects correctly
Fold napkins	*"Last night we made triangles. Let's make a different shape tonight."*	Make and identify shapes

table continued on next page

WHEN YOU AND YOUR CHILD...	YOU MIGHT SAY...	THIS HELPS YOUR CHILD LEARN TO...
Put away groceries	*"What's that?"* *"How does it feel?"* *"Does it smell?"* *"What do you think is in that can?"* *"Are there other cans on the shelf that look like this one?"*	Sort objects Count Compare objects
Wash dishes	*"What do you want to wash first, pans or plates?"* *"Are you going to start with the largest or the smallest pan?"*	Understand time sequences Understand sizes and shapes
Arrange toys by type	*"Which toys do you want to put in the box, and which do you want on the shelf?"*	Categorize and sort objects Identify where objects are in space (beside, inside, etc.)

– 9 –
Doing What Scientists Do

You may find it encouraging to know that when your child is making messes, taking things apart, and exploring in places you would prefer left alone, he or she is really just doing what scientists do. Scientists find things out and then systematically monitor, organize, and report their findings. Preschool children learn best when they "do" science. Just like scientists, they ask questions and find answers by trying out their ideas and observing what happens.

You have been nurturing your child's sense of wonder—an interest and excitement in finding out about the world—since infancy. Infants and toddlers do the work of scientists as part of their everyday lives as they observe their surroundings, test things out, and make discoveries. Squeezing a banana, examining an earthworm, and pouring sand through a sieve are a few of the ways in which young children experiment with and observe the material world. Using all their senses—touch, sight, smell, taste, and hearing—they discover relationships of change and growth and cause and effect. Toddlers on the move want to know how things work—opening and closing doors, taking objects apart, making concoctions at the sink. And, if you are the parent of a three-year-old, you are probably living through the beginning of the "whys"—endless questions about why, what, and where things are happening and who's involved.

Children are natural scientists whose search for answers should be encouraged in preschool.

You can get an idea of how a preschool program approaches scientific studies when you visit.

In one preschool, the three-year-olds classroom has a science table filled with collections of leaves, shells, acorns, and other natural materials. These collections look dusty, and the children appear to ignore them. In the class for four-year-olds, the children have made planets and their moons out of different sized balls, which are hanging from the ceiling.

In another preschool, each classroom has a pet, and the children study what and how much food the pet eats, how much the pet grows, and when it sleeps and eats. They are keeping a class record of their observations and discoveries. Last week when it snowed, they brought snow into the classroom and watched it melt. They marked puddles with chalk after a rainstorm and talked the next day about what happened to the water.

Dusty collections do not inspire children's curiosity. And, while preschool children can get very involved in making pretty planets out of balls, they are not using scientific skills to make discoveries about the planets. Adults have to tell them what they need to know to do the project. Alternatively, at the second program, children "do" science. They observe, ask questions, and look for answers. Adults guide their investigations and assist them in finding answers. Because preschool children are natural scientists, quality programs build on what children know and are interested in to support their curiosity and growing knowledge.

What's Involved in Science

Both educators and scientists agree that science teaching and learning for young children should involve active, hands-on experiences where children acquire and use scientific skills and knowledge.

Quality preschool programs seek to develop the following skills:

Asking questions. Scientific investigations begin with people's curiosity about the natural and physical world. They ask questions. Even the youngest children come to preschool ready to be scientists. If their questions are treated seriously, children retain their interest.

Observing. Scientists observe objects and events in the environment with increasing attention to detail. Preschool children can become focused observers when they see that using their senses helps them find answers to their questions.

Predicting. Scientists try to anticipate answers to their questions based on what they know and observe. In preschool, children can talk with others to explore ideas and encourage more thinking about what will happen next.

Setting up experiments. Scientists experiment to test predictions. Preschool children can be helped to plan appropriate experiments and consider what they need to conduct the experiment. Then they have to do the experiment.

Interpreting data. Scientists organize information to help them answer their questions. In preschool, children can compare, sort, classify, and make graphs to interpret information.

Communicating information. Scientists share and discuss their discoveries in many different ways. Preschool teachers can encourage children to talk about what they have seen and done, draw pictures and diagrams, make constructions or designs, dictate findings to an adult or tape recorder, or keep written records.

In addition to scientific skills, preschoolers can begin to acquire a foundation of science concepts and knowledge from which they can build. Young children benefit from studying content that is familiar to them, because they connect new knowledge to what they already know. Thus, whether the topics studied relate to the living world (e.g., plants, animals, people); matter, motion, and energy (e.g., water, wheels and gears, balls and ramps); or the earth and environment (e.g., weather, rocks, recycling), preschool children should explore content through active investigations. The choice of particular content can be based on children's interests and what is immediately available in the environment.

What Happens in Preschool

Some preschoolers love insects and classroom pets; others want to take things apart and put them together; and still others are fascinated by balls and mazes. Your child's scientific curiosity can be stimulated in a preschool environment that encourages children to find out more in a variety of ways. These are the kinds of experiences quality preschools offer.

Children engage in scientific explorations daily. Often, children's play is a way of asking questions as they attempt to figure out how

things work. As they move and do, they are asking, "What would happen if…?" The preschool classroom has a variety of materials and objects in many parts of the room that inspire scientific explorations every day. Children can talk about their ideas and discoveries and receive feedback and encouragement from adults.

Children have many scientific tools to use. String and other tools to measure length and area, magnifying devices, eye droppers, straws, measuring cups, rain gauges, magnets, and gears are some of the many wonderful materials preschool children can use to explore their world. When these materials are available every day, children receive the message that everything is open to exploration.

Children study topics over time. Older preschoolers benefit from focusing on a particular scientific topic over several weeks or months. They can develop specific knowledge of how and why things happen by, for example, maintaining an ant farm in the classroom and observing what ants look like and do, what they need to live, and how ants work together in a community. The depth of knowledge children acquire is much more important than the number of topics studied. For example, after they have studied a living animal, they should understand or know that animals eat, sleep, and grow and have particular habits of living. With this beginning understanding, children can go on to study other animals and have a frame of reference from which to ask questions and observe.

What You Should See When You Visit

When the classroom is designed for ongoing scientific explorations and teachers encourage children to think and act like scientists, children can be scientists all day long.

The Environment

Each interest area of the classroom can be a science lab:

- **Sand and water tables:** Bowls, buckets and shovels, cookie cutters, gelatin molds, dump trucks, sticks, straws, eye droppers, muffin tins, soap, sponges, water wheels, wire whisks, egg beaters, funnels, ladles, measuring cups, and spoons are some of the materials that engage children's interest and stimulate exploration.

- **Block area**: Pictures of buildings and bridges encourage experiments with construction; labeled shelves help with sorting and classifying; scales for weighing lead to experiments with heavy and light objects.

- **Music and movement activities**: Movement exercises motivate children to explore different ways in which a body can move, and to think about space as they squeeze up or stretch to become as small or large as they can. They learn about cause and effect when they explore the sounds of musical instruments.

- **Cooking activities**: When children combine ingredients, mix, stir, heat, or chill, they learn about cause and effect and change.

- **Table toys:** Objects for sorting and classifying—cubes, small figures, shells, beads, nesting boxes, rocks, pegs, and pegboards—help children become careful observers.

- **Outdoors:** Taking science tools such as magnifiers outdoors enables children to continue their experiments in the natural world.

- **Art area:** Primary paint colors encourage experimenting to create new colors; collage materials influence studies of texture; sculpting and molding materials inspire experiments with shapes and change.

In addition to what you see in each interest area, there are many other activities that could engage children as scientists. Notice what children are doing. Children can observe scientific phenomena all day long when they:

- measure rainfall

- notice how food spoils

- talk about how a carrot changes before and after it is grated

- wash chalkboards and discuss what happens to the water

- use scientific tools and equipment to investigate—magnifying devices, eye droppers, measuring cups, magnets, gears, string, and other objects for measuring

- feed pets and notice what they eat

- make soap bubbles

- roll marbles or make a marble run

- wash hands before eating

The Teachers

Adults who notice children's play and make comments or ask questions that spur new thinking encourage children to "do" science. Listen for conversations like these.

- During clean-up time as children prepare to wipe up the finger paints from the table, a teacher could ask: "What do you think might happen if you used a wet sponge to wipe up the paint and I used a dry sponge? Let's try it." Afterwards, the teacher could follow-up by asking, "What do you notice? Why do you think that happens?"

- Observing sand play: "Which kind of sand do you think can make a bigger pile, wet or dry? Would you like to experiment?" And then, "What did you find out? Why do you think that happens?"

- During building activities: "Which wall is the strongest? Why do you think so?" And then, "How could you test the walls? What did you find out?" "I see you've picked out blocks that are all the same. How are they the same?"

- While cooking: "What happens to the mixture when you stir it?" and "How did the gelatin change from when you started making it until it was time to eat it?"

- During a walk: "What do you notice about the clouds today?" "Let's look for signs of spring and see what we can find."

Fostering children's emerging scientific thinking means allowing them to do what scientists do—find answers for themselves. When the preschool classroom and teachers engage children as scientists, they encourage a sense of wonder and a desire to question and experiment.

What You Should *Not* See

- Projects that only some children get to do while the others watch and wait.

- Teachers conducting science experiments while children watch quietly.

- A science area or table that is little used and uninteresting.

Questions to Ask

- What science topics are children exploring?

- Do you have pets in the classroom?

- How do you decide what science projects to do?

- Do children do cooking?

- What do you suggest parents do at home?

What Happens at Home

You can be a scientist with your child as part of your everyday activities. Think about the many things you do together that offer opportunities for scientific thinking.

WHEN YOU AND YOUR CHILD…	YOU MIGHT SAY…	THIS HELPS YOUR CHILD LEARN TO…
Prepare and cook simple foods	*"Feel this peanut butter. How does it feel to you?"* *"Look at the popcorn before it popped and look at it after. How is it different?"* *"Remember how we scrambled the eggs? What did we do first? Next? Last?"*	Describe how things feel Notice cause and effect Describe how things change Understand time sequence
Do water play activities together using empty plastic containers of different sizes	*"How does it sound when you put that empty bottle under water?"* *"Do all bottles sound the same when you put them under water?"* *"Which top fits on this tiny bottle? On this larger bottle?"*	Learn about volume Arrange objects in a series from smallest to largest
Experiment with objects that sink and float in the tub	*"What do you think will happen—will this sink or float?"* *"What happens if you push it to the bottom of the bathtub and let it go?"* *"What happens if you fill it with water?"*	Explore and identify characteristics of objects Make discoveries and experiment

– 10 –
Finding Out about the World

If social studies is understood as the study of people—how people live, work, get along with others, solve problems, shape and are shaped by their surroundings—then social studies learning begins at birth. The people preschoolers know best are themselves, their families, and the people in their communities. Young children begin to learn social studies by forming relationships, learning to communicate, and exploring the world around them. As they do these things, they are forming understandings that relate to geography, civics, and history.

Your child has been a geographer since infancy—exploring physical space by crawling, climbing, digging, and splashing. When he figured out how to get from one room to another, to maneuver a toy car around objects, or to "hide" a treasure, he was using beginning mapping skills. The social skills learned being a member of the family and then a part of a group in preschool—how to communicate with others to have wants and needs met—were beginning civics. Civics learning continues when you take your child to the supermarket, the doctor, the hardware store, the shoe store, and the playground and when you talk about people at work and play. And although you may not have thought about it, you teach your child history every time you talk about how much she has grown, what she can do this week that she couldn't last week, and the everyday events and routines that you've established at home. Children learn about time from the daily, predictable routines you establish—a story before bedtime, washing hands before meals, brushing teeth twice a day.

A good preschool will build on and extend your child's learning about social studies. However, you may find significant differences in the way programs address social studies topics.

In one program, each preschool classroom studies a theme a week. Sometimes it is holiday-related—Columbus Day, Halloween, Thanksgiving, Valentine's Day. At other times, children study colors or shapes or topics such as me and my family, transportation, or dental hygiene.

In another program, the teachers and children spend much more time on many fewer topics. During November, they studied their families, investigating where they bought food, what they prepared for Thanksgiving, and how. Later in the year, they began a study of stores in their neighborhood beginning with a visit to the nearby bakery.

What's the difference between "theme-a-week" learning and in-depth learning through first-hand explorations and play? The first program aims to increase the number of facts children "know." Expecting children to memorize facts about explorers or pilgrims with little or no connection to their own lives is not likely to hold much meaning for preschoolers. On the other hand, when learning is connected to children's lives—to what their families do on a holiday or what they see happening across the street with huge trucks and machinery—their curiosity is challenged. To get tangibly involved in their own learning, the subject matter for preschoolers has to be what they can see and touch.

What's Involved in Learning Social Studies

Children in preschool can learn about social studies firsthand. Belonging to a classroom community offers opportunities to live, work, and share with others. In such an environment, children learn the rudiments for living in a democratic society. Here are some of the social studies concepts children can begin to explore during the preschool years.

Spatial or geographic thinking. Geographical thinking begins with understanding space, becoming aware of the characteristics of the places where you live, and thinking about that place's location in relation to other places. In preschool, children can study the physical characteristics of their world—the sandbox area, the slides, the swings, and the grassy area by the tree—and talk about how to navigate in it. They can talk about mapping by discussing directions—how to get to the bathroom, the playground, the carpool line. They can recreate their neighborhood in the block area and draw or paint maps of places they go. The goal is for children to begin to understand that maps represent actual places.

People and how they live. Learning about people means recognizing physical characteristics; noticing similarities and differences in habits, homes, and work; thinking about family structures and roles; and recognizing how people rely on each other for goods and services. Preschool children can begin to explore these ideas by studying themselves and their families and thinking about rules in the classroom and how they help people live together and get along.

People and the environment. People affect the environment by changing it—building cities, making roads, building a highway or dam—and by protecting it—cleaning up a park, recycling, saving some green space from development. In preschool, children can explore the area near their homes or school to learn more about their local environment.

People and the past. While an adult understanding of chronological time is essential to understanding history, preschool children are focused on the here and now. They can begin to learn about time in relation to themselves. They can talk about their daily schedule, what they did yesterday, and what they will do tomorrow. Preschool children love to consider what they can do now that they couldn't do when they were "babies." They can appreciate stories about other times and places if the topics are relevant to their own experiences.

What Happens in Preschool

Children are eager to learn more about the people and places they see every day. Social studies teaching should build on children's natural curiosity to explore the world around them. They can learn to observe carefully, collect information, compare facts, and build understanding. Quality preschools pay attention to children's stages of development and to the importance of developing social skills. Here are some characteristics of high-quality programs.

Children learn social studies as part of everyday life in the classroom. Preschool itself provides an important social studies experience. As children play side-by-side—sometimes alone and sometimes with others—they learn to share, take turns, and cooperate. Children also benefit when teachers model and talk about appropriate behavior. In addition, discussions about the need for rules—what it would be like if everyone grabbed their lunch at the same time, if no one cleaned up, if everyone wanted to be in the art area at once—help children become aware of the needs of group living and how decisions can be made. When the classroom functions as a community, children practice responsible citizenship every day. They make choices, learn to accept different points of view and different ways of thinking, and are encouraged and taught how to treat others respectfully.

Children have concrete materials and objects related to their own lives to encourage investigations. Preschool children engaged in first-hand social studies research need materials. Playing with dolls, pots and pans, menus, and checkbooks, for example, allows children to try out different family roles and responsibilities. Props and accessories, such as hammers, stethoscopes, cash registers, and hats, give children opportunities to play the roles of people they see in their lives.

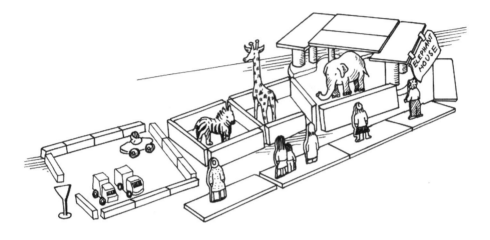

Children have opportunities to investigate topics over time.
Older preschoolers are ready to study topics or themes over time
and in-depth so that they can become "experts." Their curiosity
extends beyond themselves to include others—they want to know
about the other children in their class and their families. They ask
questions about the neighborhood they see each day. Gradually,
they begin to question how things are made, how they work, and
who makes them. In quality programs, the topics chosen reflect
what teachers know about the community and the interests of the
children. And most importantly, the topics chosen allow children to
be in control—to be the investigators themselves rather than depending on adults or books for the necessary information.

Study topics or themes begin with what children know and see
every day. A program in Alaska might study salmon fishing and
what tools people use to catch fish. Another program located near
food stores and bakeries might study bread making and bakeries.
Children can then have firsthand experiences that enable them to
construct their own knowledge. They talk about what they see, act

out their understandings of what people do, and build objects and materials that relate to the study.

Study topics can grow from unexpected events that offer rich opportunities for exploration. Suppose, for example, a construction project begins near your child's preschool. The children see large machinery brought in to dig the foundation; they see pipes being laid and foundation walls going up. Because of the children's enthusiasm, the teacher incorporates a construction project into the curriculum by making regular visits to the site and encouraging children to talk about the work being done and the changes they notice. The interest areas then encourage children to use their growing understanding of the topic to express their ideas as they play. Below are things you might see in the classroom interest areas during this study of a construction site:

- **Block area:** Pictures of how buildings are constructed; bulldozers, tubes, backhoes, ramps, derricks, and construction workers.

- **House corner:** Hard hat, lunch boxes, carpenter aprons, work boots, and work shirts.

- **Library:** Books that illustrate construction work; photographs of the construction site to illustrate the changes; stories the children have dictated about the project.

- **Table toys:** Construction materials such as Legos® and table blocks.

- **Art area:** A group mural of the building under construction.

What You Should See When You Visit

If the class is studying a particular topic at the time of your visit, you should see evidence of this in interest areas as we described earlier with the construction site example. Notice what materials are in the block area to spur children's thinking or whether the dramatic play area reflects a particular theme.

In addition to specific materials or activities in interest areas, social studies learning can be a part of everyday life in the classroom.

- In taking attendance, children think about who is here and who isn't and why they might be absent.

- Older preschoolers work together on projects, such as making a mural, planning an event, recreating the neighborhood in the block corner, or preparing a meal.

- Because members of a community care about one another, children write or draw pictures to their classmates who are ill.

- Teachers and children together talk about how to clean up, how to share chores, and what rules are needed. For example, interest areas may be organized so that only a certain number of children can play there at a time. The children talk about such rules and whether or not they are necessary.

- Children begin to learn about chronological time and the passage of time as they think about the daily or weekly schedule—what they do after lunch or before snack and what they did together earlier in the week or month.

Children can be exposed to and learn about many aspects of social studies in classrooms that call attention to ways the people in a community live together.

What You Should *Not* See

- Displays that are mostly commercially made or adult made.

- Activities directed for the whole group at one time, with children expected to answer test-like questions posed by the teachers. (What color are apples? What color are pumpkins?)

- A classroom that functions more like a dictatorship than a democracy.

Questions to Ask

- How do you generate the rules for the classroom?

- What expectations do you have for children to clean up?

- What social studies topics do children explore during the year?

- How do you select topics?

- Do you take trips with the children to learn about the community?

- What trips are planned?

- What do you suggest parents do at home?

What Happens at Home

Social studies research can be a part of what you do together at home.

WHEN YOU AND YOUR CHILD...	YOU MIGHT SAY...	THIS HELPS YOUR CHILD LEARN TO...
Discuss everyday experiences in your neighborhood	*"I wonder what's making that loud sound?"* *"Why do you think the police put on that loud siren and those flashing lights?"* *"Where do you think they are going?"*	Describe people and objects Understand roles people play in society
Wash the car together	*"Want to help me wash the car?"* *"Here, rub this soapy sponge on the front fender while I work on the hood. Next we'll rinse the car with water."*	Share in household chores Cooperate with others Understand time sequences.
Clean up toys	*"Let's put all the cars together, then the people. Now we can put the cars in one box and the people in another so you can find them tomorrow."*	Share responsibility for caring for belongings Organize objects systematically

– 11 –
Creating through the Arts

Art is a language for communicating ideas, information, and feelings. Experiences in the arts enable children to think about, organize, and express themselves in ways that do not rely on words and numbers. Children who use art materials–to paint, draw, mold, weave, design, and construct–and who explore music and movement activities– singing, playing instruments, listening to music, moving to music, creating puppet shows, and pretending–are growing socially, emotionally, cognitively, and physically.

At home, you have often encouraged different aspects of the arts, depending on your own interests. If you like to sing, you have probably sung to your child since infancy. You and your child may have listened to music together, and responded differently to different kinds of music. Perhaps you've enjoyed tapping out rhythms as your child bangs on a toy drum. You may like to draw, paint, or make crafts, and you've involved your child in these activities. And, if you have been encouraging your child to dance with you or put on shows, then he or she may be comfortable with those forms of artistic expression. Although children's development as artists is not automatic, when they have opportunities, materials, encouragement, and time to explore, they can create at surprisingly high levels.

As you visit preschool programs, look carefully at the kinds of art experiences children are offered. Some have nothing to do with helping children develop creativity and may, in fact, reinforce adult ideas of what art should look like.

In one program, the artwork on the walls all looks the same—mostly shapes drawn by adults and decorated by children. The bulletin boards are covered with cheerful pictures or signs made by adults to look child-like or with commercially-made pictures. In the art area, several children are pasting triangles on orange paper to make Halloween pumpkins.

In another program, a group of children is working in the art area with a large container of collage materials. The teacher talks with the children about how the materials feel—soft, rough, crunchy, smooth, silky, wet. The children then explore different combinations and glue them on cardboard. As they play, a child begins a spontaneous song about the "squishy" bubble wrap, and the teacher adds on a verse about the "bumpy" corrugated paper.

Each program approaches art activities with a different focus. In the first program, the object of the activity is for children to produce finished products to take home to parents and to decorate the walls. Teachers design the projects, and children follow directions. In the second program, the emphasis is on children playing with materials to make discoveries about how things look and feel, and creating their own designs. Because the teacher knows that children develop musical "language" by using it, she encourages spontaneous singing during many different activities, all day long.

What's Involved in the Arts

Many people feel if they are not "good" at music or drawing or dancing, they can't effectively promote their child's artistic development. Research indicates, however, that artistic development is very much influenced by exposure and cultivation, not just by inborn talent. Research also shows that singing and listening to music encourages brain development; in addition, musical expression is another form of intelligence. Thus, children who have opportunities to explore different kinds of artistic expression and are guided in their development show higher levels of achievement than children who lack these opportunities.

Visual arts. The visual arts in preschool include painting, drawing, making collages, modeling with clays or other materials, building, making puppets, weaving and stitching, and printmaking with stamps, blocks, or rubbings. Children benefit from being offered opportunities to work with different kinds of paint and paper; draw with crayons, markers, and chalk; put things together with paste and glue; cut with scissors; mold playdough; and clean up with mops, sponges, and brooms. The more exposure children have to diverse materials—and to adults who talk about different ways to use the materials—the more able children become to express their ideas through the visual arts.

Music. Music literacy develops when children can listen to and interact with many kinds of music. This means programs should provide opportunities to play with music materials and instruments, to learn songs and make up songs, to listen to recordings, and to talk about sounds. When preschool children explore instruments on their own, create melodies, learn songs as a group, and make up songs, they develop awareness of different kinds of music and become comfortable with different ways of musical expression.

Movement. Young children are natural movers—they "think with their bodies" well before they think with words. When children are encouraged to use their bodies to express ideas, to respond to different rhythm patterns, and to vary their responses to different musical phrases, they learn about the body's ability to move and use time and space in many different ways.

Drama. Drama is telling a story through action or dialogue. Preschool children recognize that movement can communicate messages and represent actions. During the preschool years, children learn through pretend play to pantomime actions such as eating, swimming, or driving a car, and learn to play the roles of parent, firefighter, or a superhero.

What Happens in Preschool

Most children come to preschool having spent time scribbling at the kitchen table or on the floor, "messing around" with finger-paint and playdough, banging on pots and pans, hearing recordings, and singing a few familiar songs. In a quality preschool program, however, play in the arts is an essential component. Such play should be based on a true understanding of what is involved in developing children's self-expression and appreciation for the arts. Look for three key indicators that the arts are valued by a preschool program.

Children have multiple opportunities every day to explore and create in the arts. Most preschool children do not know what it is they are going to draw or make before they do it. Free exploration and enough time are essential to art, music, movement, and drama experiences. Obviously, this means that teachers must provide the space and allow time for children to try out their ideas, ask questions, and be guided to notice possibilities or other ways of doing things. Sometimes children need to play alone as they explore (for example, trying out a musical instrument or painting at the easel); sometimes they can be in a small group (for example, experimenting with different movements to music or planning a puppet show); and sometimes children should be part of the whole class (as in singing a song or chant).

Children have a variety of art materials, musical instruments, and musical recordings to explore. Doing art requires both repeated opportunities and a variety of materials. In the visual arts, you should see materials and objects for painting and drawing, cutting and gluing, molding and building, weaving and stitching. Children can explore materials as they talk about how to use them. As children decide how to choose materials, they learn to observe carefully and plan their work. Similarly, children need to hear a great deal of music and experiment with musical instruments to learn how to make sounds and change sounds. As they try out different ways to move their bodies to music, they learn about patterns and rhythm.

Children have opportunities to look at, listen to, and respond to works of art created by others and to talk about what they see and hear. When children look at works of great painters and sculptors, hear recordings of songs and symphonies, watch experienced dancers, and listen to musicians, they form opinions about what they like and dislike and learn to respond to artistic expression. Learning to observe and listen carefully and then share observations and experiences is as important for artistic development as it is for becoming better readers and writers or scientific thinkers.

What You Should See When You Visit

Preschool children can grow as artists as they play with many materials throughout the classroom and are encouraged and guided by teachers who see these activities as important.

The Environment

We have described all the different materials that might be available for the visual arts in an art area. These are examples of what you should look for in other interest areas:

- **House corner:** Paper and markers or crayons for drawing, a tape recorder with musical favorites to put "baby" to sleep, a musical instrument to use as part of the play in this area.

- **Library:** Books with pictures of the works of great artists; recordings of different kinds of music that individual children can listen to.

- **Music and movement area:** An assortment of musical
  instruments such as drums, rhythm sticks, cymbals,
  kazoos, tambourines, triangles, shakers, bells, xylophones,
  and wood blocks, many of which can come from different
  cultures around the world; materials to encourage movement and pretend activities, such as colorful scarves or
  crepe streamers, grass skirts, and pieces of fabric to use as
  makeshift costumes.

In addition to what you see going on in these interest areas,
look for effective teachers who encourage children to develop as
artists and musicians as part of many daily activities. Your visit may
come at a time when children are:

- singing as they switch from one activity to another

- making up songs about things that happen during the day

- solving conflicts by role-playing problems

- choosing expressive movements as they go outside or
  come to the circle area

- listening to music during the day

- talking about professional art work in the classroom

The Teachers

Teachers help children go beyond exploring art to creating it. As children participate in art activities, the teacher influences their growth and development by responding to their work and engaging them in conversations about what they are doing. Here are the kinds of things you want to hear teachers say:

- Describing what they see: "I see so many shapes in your painting." "You covered the whole paper." "You put the same things on each side of the paper—what an interesting pattern." "You made up words to that new song we learned." "You've made up a rhythm with two pats on the drum and then a bell sound."

- Talking about the process: "How did you make this?" "You are really pounding that playdough." "You made some lines go up and down and some go from side to side."

- Asking questions that encourage new thinking: "What are some ways you could fill up this paper?" How is this collage different from the first one you made?" What are some ways to make these stick together?" "Which music is better for getting ready to go to sleep and which would you like to hear when you wake up?"

- Using words to encourage and support children's efforts: "You worked for a long time on those two paintings. Which would you like to hang on the wall?" "Would you like to make a recording of the song you made up with Joey?"

Children become keener observers and listeners when teachers help them focus their attention carefully. Listen for conversations that begin:

- "Suppose you were talking to me on the telephone. How would you describe this mobile to me so that I would know just what it looks like without seeing it?"

- "Can you find a line in that drawing and follow it with your finger?"
- "How does this music make you want to move?"
- "Let's see if we can clap to the beat of this music."

The arts in high quality preschool programs cannot just involve some drawing, painting, and a few songs and finger plays. If children are to have rich opportunities to develop artistic expression—just as they develop literacy—then programs have to offer much more to encourage each child's optimal growth and development.

What You Should *Not* See

- Art projects that use precut shapes or designs for product oriented projects.
- Coloring books, or teachers correcting or completing children's art.
- Limited displays of only the "best" artwork.
- Always directing how children should move to music.

Questions to Ask

- How much time do children spend each day in a creative art experience?
- How do you decide what materials to make available in the art area?
- What kinds of music do the children listen to?
- What songs are children learning?
- Do you look at the works of any great artists?
- When do children explore movement activities?

What Happens at Home

Your interests are likely to determine what you emphasize in your home. Here are some examples.

WHEN YOU AND YOUR CHILD...	YOU MIGHT SAY...	THIS HELPS YOUR CHILD LEARN TO...
Go to the supermarket	*"Let's make up a song about what we're doing now. A shopping we will go, a shopping we will go!"*	Understand music as a way to represent ideas Recognize that music can be a part of daily activities
Set the table	*"Would you like to make a picture to put on grandma's plate to welcome her?"*	Do things for others Make decisions about what materials to use and ideas to express
Listen to music together	*"This music makes me want to clap. Let's do it together."*	Become aware of rhythm and patterns Follow a beat
Look at a picture together	*"Where do you think the child is going in this picture?"* *"Can you think of where he is coming from?"*	Observe closely to get ideas and form opinions
Make a card for Grandma	*"I'll write down your words after you finish your picture."*	Express ideas through drawings and words

– 12 –
Thinking Ahead to Kindergarten

As you face the task of choosing the best preschool program for your child, the thought of kindergarten probably seems a long way off. You may wonder, therefore, why you should be thinking of it now as you are making decisions about preschool. We offer two compelling reasons.

First, transitions are big events for young children. The more continuity they can have during these early years, the better. Many preschools—including child care programs—now include or are connected with kindergartens. If your child is having the kinds of preschool experiences we describe in this book, and the program continues through kindergarten, you may want to extend the time he or she spends in this nurturing and enriching environment. Practical considerations—such as convenient geographic location, younger siblings who are attending preschool, or tuition costs—may also influence your decision whether or not to keep your child in the same program through kindergarten.

Second, at kindergarten age, children still need a continuation of what they have been doing in preschool more than they need a formal academic program. Unfortunately today, many kindergarten classrooms look more like rooms for older children. Interest areas—the blocks, dramatic play props, toys, art, sand and water tables—are usually fewer, less elaborate, or nonexistent. There may be limited opportunities for children to make choices and more teacher-directed activities with art media or other materials. Children may be required to sit and complete paper and pencil tasks for long periods of time. The expectations of what children need to learn in kindergarten have been raised inappropriately—and the result is that more children experience difficulty or failure, or are forced to repeat kindergarten.

There are elementary schools that do offer appropriate kindergarten programs. We therefore suggest that as you look at preschools, you visit the elementary school your child will attend. Find out if the school offers or coordinates with a preschool program. Spend some time in the kindergarten, talk with the principal, and ask some of the questions we have outlined in this book. Many elementary schools adhere to the philosophy we espouse, and their kindergarten program may be a good one for your child. On the other hand, if you discover a very formal academic kindergarten program in your local elementary school, you should consider your choices. In some school districts, you may have a choice about which school your child attends, so you may want to visit several schools. You could also join with other parents who have similar concerns about the school your child will attend to advocate for more appropriate expectations and practices. Alternatively, you can select a preschool like the ones we describe in this book that includes kindergarten. We hope the information in this chapter will be helpful in whatever choice you make.

What Kindergarten Should Be Like

Children in kindergarten generally range in age from four-and-a-half-year-olds to six-year-olds. At this age, they are closer in their development to preschoolers than they are to primary grade children. Therefore, a good kindergarten program should look more like a good preschool than like first grade.[11] Organizations like the National Association for the Education of Young Children (NAEYC) clearly support this idea. In their book, *Kindergarten Policies: What Is Best for Children?* NAEYC makes a strong statement.

> *A great deal of quite conclusive research over half a century tells us that kindergarten-aged children still think like younger children; they think differently, see the world differently, act differently, and have different skills than children of 7 or 8...The kindergarten year is one more important year in a child's lengthy process of growing up. It is not developmentally helpful, or in the long run a success, to push and rush children through it.[12]*

The kindergarten program you choose for your child should follow the practices described throughout this book. Such a program strengthens children's social, emotional, and physical skills, and provides varied opportunities for children to explore reading and writing, discover mathematical relationships, do what scientists do, find out about the world, and create through the arts. In this type of kindergarten, you would see children talking with each other, exploring materials, solving problems together, and in general, deeply involved in and excited by their work.

However, you should also see some differences between preschool and kindergarten. More focused time should be spent on early reading and writing, mathematical thinking, and long-term studies. Here are some things to look for:

- **Meeting times:** Expect the schedule to include several times during the day for the whole group to gather for discussions about a topic the class is studying, resolve a problem in the classroom, participate in a lesson planned by the teacher, and share work they have completed.

- **Work times:** Look for one or two planned periods—depending on the length of the kindergarten day—for focused work on reading and writing or math tasks. These work times might center around a math task such as making and repeating patterns, sorting and classifying objects and comparing them on a graph, writing and drawing in personal journals, finding words that sound alike in a poem, or looking at books. You should see children working in small groups or individually, and a teacher going from group to group. If you visit during a meeting time, you may observe a teacher leading a meeting in which each group presents their work to the whole class.

- **Long-term studies:** Look for evidence of long-term projects. By the time they are in kindergarten, children are ready to explore the kinds of studies we described in science and social studies but in greater depth, perhaps for several weeks or even months.

The focused time children spend on tasks and extended studies of topics that interest them makes kindergarten a bridge between preschool and elementary school. But how will you know when your child is ready to move to kindergarten?

Determining Readiness for Kindergarten

As your child approaches kindergarten age, you may wonder whether he or she is ready for this next step. This question is sometimes resolved by holding children back or relying on readiness tests to assess whether a child has acquired the prerequisite skills and knowledge to do well in kindergarten. Each of these responses is an accommodation to kindergarten programs that set unrealistic expectations for children—expectations that are inappropriate and lead many children to experience difficulty or failure in kindergarten. We stand against such program practices that pressure children, instigate failure, and instill feelings of incompetence in young children.

Entry Age for Kindergarten

The cut-off date (the date by which a child must reach age five) to enter kindergarten varies across the country from June 1st to December 31st, with September 1st being the most common (adopted by eighteen states). This means that depending on their birth dates, children in some states may enter kindergarten at four-and-a-half, and in others, possibly not until they are almost five-and-a-half. Such a range in the entry age for kindergarten can be very confusing, especially if you know that the rationale for pushing back the date is to ensure that children can "handle" the curriculum. If your child's fifth birthday is near the cut-off date in your state, you may be tempted to keep your child out an extra year to be sure he or she will be successful in school. This is what some parents are doing.

Keep in mind that if you hold your child out of kindergarten, the real problem—inappropriate curriculum expectations—still exists. In addition, though your child may be better equipped to handle a more formal academic program a year later, socially and emotionally he or she will be older than most other children in the class for the duration of his or her school career. We encourage you to think carefully about when to enroll your child in kindergarten, recognizing that there may be circumstances in which you feel your child is not socially or emotionally ready for even an appropriate kindergarten program. However, if you feel the curriculum is unrealistic and potentially damaging to your child, and you are unable to change it (we'll say more about this later in the chapter), then selecting another program for kindergarten may be preferable, if it is feasible for you. We will give you some guidelines for assessing your child's readiness for kindergarten later in this chapter.

Readiness Tests

Readiness tests are another commonly used approach to determine whether children are eligible to enter kindergarten. But readiness tests have several problems. For one, they test only discrete skills and knowledge, and we know there is more to readiness than whether a child knows the alphabet, colors, and various other concepts. Additionally, using readiness tests with young children is not a particularly reliable way to assess what they know and can do.[13] Many factors affect how children respond to a test: whether they understand how tests work; how much sleep they had the night before; how they interpret the question or task; and even what time of day the test is given. NAEYC explains:

> *Tests cannot tell us: what thinking processes children use to solve problems; whether children's curiosity is being enhanced; what strategies children use to get along with each other; whether children can appreciate beauty and diversity in the world around them; how kind children are to others; whether children are persistent in real situations; or whether children have a growing sense of responsibility for themselves and others. Tests do not, and cannot, measure the broad scope of what children are learning.[14]*

A single test, if it's a good test and used appropriately, still can only give a small sampling of the skills and abilities that children exhibit in a given testing situation on a given day.

Rather than using readiness tests, schools based on best practices recognize that every child brings to kindergarten a wealth of individual skills, knowledge, and experience, as well as a "readiness" to learn more. These schools accept their responsibility to be "ready" for all children by providing appropriate instruction that meets the needs of each child. They recognize that all children do not learn everything at the same pace and do not judge children in terms of what they "can do" or "can't do." Teachers observe children over time, gather information about their abilities in all developmental and subject areas, and consider how to help them to progress with all of their skills. This is true whether a child has many basic skills and concepts yet to be mastered or has many advanced skills and is ripe for enrichment opportunities. A kindergarten program that reflects recent research and best practices uses a thorough approach to determine what children know and can do, rather than simply a readiness test or a one-time checklist.

We conclude that the use of readiness tests to determine kindergarten entry should be abandoned. Instead of testing children to see if they are "ready" for kindergarten, we should do everything we can to give children a good start and to be sure that schools provide experiences that are appropriate for children at each stage of their development. Until this happens, if you are in a school system that requires readiness tests, talk with the school to find out what is involved and if there are other ways they assess children's readiness for kindergarten.

A More Accurate Way to Determine Readiness

In 1990, President Bush and the state governors established as the first National Education Goal that, "By the year 2000, all children in America will start school ready to learn." A technical planning group for the National Education Goals Panel, which was charged with developing a way to define and assess readiness, identified five important factors, or areas of development, that should be considered.[15]

- Physical well-being and motor development (e.g., gross- and fine-motor skills, physical fitness)

- Social and emotional development (e.g., ability to form and sustain relationships with adults and friends, show empathy and sensitivity to others, cooperate with peers, listen to other points of view, express feelings appropriately, have a positive self-concept)

- Approaches towards learning (e.g., openness to and curiosity about new tasks, persistence and attentiveness, imagination)

- Language usage (e.g., verbal skills such as listening, speaking, questioning, and emerging literacy, such as print awareness, story sense, and writing process)

- General knowledge about the world (e.g., mathematical, social, and physical knowledge)

Selecting the type of preschool program described in this book and offering a broad variety of experiences at home are the best ways to help your child build a solid foundation for learning in kindergarten and beyond. When the time for kindergarten nears, talk with your child's preschool teacher. Together, you can assess whether your child

- has the verbal skills to communicate ideas, engage in conversations, and respond to questions

- is curious, is eager to explore, asks questions, and seeks answers

- can make friends, relates to others in positive ways, and cooperates

- can control impulses and postpone gratification

- recognizes emotions in others and shows empathy

- is an active learner, able to sustain play and complete tasks

Using these measures, you can more reliably judge whether your child is ready to move on from preschool. If your child is already reading, an appropriate kindergarten program should provide enriching activities that extend your child's experience and skills. On the other hand, your child may not recognize all the letters of the alphabet or count accurately to twenty, but he or she may have good physical coordination and the strong social skills needed to thrive in a developmentally appropriate kindergarten program. Don't be persuaded to keep your child out of kindergarten based on what he or she doesn't yet know.

Becoming an Advocate for Your Child's Education

It may seem like an overwhelming task to choose a preschool program and also to make sure your child will have a good kindergarten program. Like many parents, you may feel you have little to say about the policies and practices of elementary schools. In fact, by starting early and becoming involved, you can make a difference in the experiences your child has in school.

The first step is to become informed about the latest research and recommendations about good practice in early childhood education. Reading this book is a step in that direction, and we have listed other good resources in appendix D. Next, join with other parents who share your views, and make your opinions known. Advocacy is every citizen's right. Contact the principal of the school or schools in your neighborhood, and offer to become involved. Set up a meeting to talk about the curriculum, share your concerns, and begin a dialogue. A knowledgeable and involved parent is a great asset to a school. You will be surprised at how much influence a group of concerned parents can have on a school.

Conclusion

The White House Conference on Early Childhood Development concluded in April 1997, that what happens to a child in the earliest years affects how well he or she learns for a lifetime. We all know the early years of schooling are formative ones. During this time, children decide whether learning is inherently interesting and worthy of effort—or boring and tedious. It is also the time when children build a sense of self and discover whether they are competent learners. These years are the most important for developing the social skills that are essential for a happy and productive life—in school and beyond. Selecting a good preschool and kindergarten program for your child is one of the most important decisions you will make about your child's education.

We began by talking about the challenges involved in selecting a good preschool for your child. We hope that this book has taken some of the confusion and worry out of the process. Empowered with information and a vision of high-quality preschool programs, we hope you feel ready to sort through the conflicting messages of different preschools and to find a program that meets your child's needs. The simple answer, "earlier is better," is not right and not in children's best long-term interests. You don't have to choose between an academic focus and play. Both are possible if teachers honor children's capacity to learn through stimulating play experiences.

Guided rather than pushed, all children can feel capable in school and excited about learning.

This does not mean that every day in preschool can be a perfect one for your child if only you choose the right program. Even the best programs sometimes fall short. What's more, you'll need to make tradeoffs involving your convenience, personal values, and the needs of your child and family. We hope this book has helped you balance the factors that compete in a thoughtful way.

Our final word of advice is to trust yourself. You know your child best, and you want the best for your child. You also recognize that the benefits of making a good choice, while important, are not the only factors that will influence your child's life. The time you spend with your child is more important and valuable than anything else. Take time to play with your child, talk together, and read wonderful books every day. Those experiences and the positive relationship you develop with your child will be the strongest foundation for success in school and in life.

Appendixes A–F

Endnotes

Index

A Note from Teaching Strategies, Inc.

– Appendix A –
Understanding the Preschool Child

As a parent, you have undoubtedly noticed how your child's needs change over time. Remember when you had to do everything for your child? Later, as your child became more mobile and able to get around and communicate, you adapted and changed your role, encouraging him or her to be more independent and make discoveries. This approach of adapting to meet a child's changing needs also works in the classroom, and for this reason, we place so much emphasis on understanding the preschool child.

In high-quality preschool programs, teachers understand child development and how children learn. They base their practices on this knowledge, just as you have done. As a result, good teachers can continually expose children to new and challenging experiences that build their confidence and their skills.

What Two- to Five-Year-Olds Are Like

During these early childhood years, children are learning to trust others outside their families, to gain independence and self-control, and to take initiative and assert themselves in socially acceptable ways. At the same time, they are learning about their world by observing their surroundings and finding out what happens when they interact with materials and other people. Their language skills grow enormously—from age two, when they may have a vocabulary of one to two hundred, to age six, when they add between eight and fourteen thousand words! They develop the ability to talk about their observations and experiences as they explore their surroundings. Their environment becomes larger and richer as they learn to understand others and express their ideas more effectively. While all this cognitive development is occurring, preschoolers are also changing physically. They are strengthening their large muscles and learning to use them to run, skip, jump, hop, and climb. They need physical activity all day long in order to thrive. At the same time, preschoolers are developing fine motor skills more slowly. It is important to remember that an individual child's development does not follow an even course across all areas.

The Transition from Two to Three

The independent nature of two-year-olds is captured in some of their favorite phrases: "Mine," "No," and "Me do it." They are very busy people and assert themselves as a matter of course as they explore and figure things out for themselves. Among the many physical achievements of this transition year is learning to use the toilet. Two-year-olds are naturally curious and interested in other people. They can be very caring of one another one minute then become angry and aggressive soon afterwards. Twos tend to have very strong feelings and often don't know how to express them. But they are fascinated with words, and as they approach three, they usually can use words to communicate their needs, express their feelings, and even comfort themselves.

More and more, two-year-olds are enrolled in organized care programs. We are concerned that many preschool programs designed for three- to five-year-olds offer two-year-olds the same program they offer the older children. This is inappropriate and not in the best interests of young children. Twos benefit from a program that respects their needs for individual play and flexible scheduling, that allows plenty of time for the routines of their lives—taking jackets on and off, using the bathroom, snacking, and resting. Two-year-olds are just beginning to be interested in playing with other children, but this interest does not include sharing toys or materials. Because they have short attention spans, they are generally unable to sit in groups for any length of time. As children turn three, they are much more ready for focused play in small groups where they learn to take turns, share, and listen to one another.

Three-Year-Olds

Just think about what three-year-olds can now do with their bodies—walk quickly, run, climb stairs, jump off steps, and ride a tricycle. They can usually get undressed (but not dressed), begin to draw simple shapes, build towers with blocks, pour from a small pitcher, string beads, and put pegs in a pegboard. And, if you're the parent of a three-year-old, you're probably living through the beginning of the "whys." Many three-year-olds are beginning to play well next to others, rather than "with" others, and together they love being "silly."

In preschool, three-year-olds need a carefully planned environment with sufficient materials to explore and many duplicates so that sharing is kept to a minimum. They are ready for more sustained play. With skillful adult involvement, their social interactions will be positive, and language growth will be encouraged. Threes need time to move and many opportunities to practice new skills and feel competent about what they can do.

Four-Year-Olds

Fours are so proud when they can skip and climb on a jungle gym, build complex structures, and draw recognizable people. They consider themselves very independent about dressing and undressing, brushing teeth, and taking care of their needs. Fours have become so skilled with language that they can now tease others as well as sing songs and recite rhymes and finger plays. They tell stories about things that happen to them and introduce new vocabulary into their sentences every day. This age usually marks the beginning of the kind of give-and-take play that is required when children really play together rather than next to one another. But this kind of play can also be frustrating, and fours get angry because they don't always have the verbal skills or the ability to resolve conflicts easily.

Fours thrive in a preschool program that recognizes their need to be stimulated with interesting and challenging learning opportunities. They still need to explore with their hands and eyes to learn, but they crave real opportunities to take initiative and puzzle things out on their own. Four-year-olds want to learn about topics of personal interest: their families, the foods they eat, and activities that are common to their lives, such as going to the supermarket, to the shoe store, or to the apple orchard. In the classroom, they need large blocks of uninterrupted time to work with the materials in each play area.

Five-Year-Olds

Five-year-olds revel in their newly acquired skills. With their high energy levels, they can run, hop, jump rope, climb, maybe even swim or ride a bike. They can hammer a nail, use scissors carefully, draw people, and print some letters of the alphabet. Fives also want to please and show affection, so it's a great time for the important adults in their lives. At the same time, fives are very focused on themselves. They learn by doing things themselves rather than by watching or listening to instructions. They are more experienced at sharing but still find it difficult to do so; understanding another person's point of view remains a challenge. Imaginative play is an important part of their lives, and they sometimes confuse fantasy and reality.

Although fives can sound very mature, they still need a great deal of adult support and guidance to negotiate with friends and make transitions from one activity to another. They are still very concrete thinkers who learn from what they can see and touch. Most five-year-olds are not yet able to use their eyes truly efficiently or easily scan a page from left to right. Letter reversals are very common at this stage and are to be expected rather than corrected. Because most fives cannot yet distinguish subtle differences in sounds, they still like to be read to, but they should not be pushed to figure out sounds and letters on their own.

– APPENDIX B –
Special Needs and Inclusion

All parents want to be sure their children are getting enough attention to benefit from preschool experiences and to be happy and secure in the program. However, you may be concerned that your child is not doing well in some developmental areas or seems far behind others in the same general age group. Should you be troubled by these concerns, don't hesitate to seek information and guidance. You can ask your pediatrician or your child's teacher whether their observations match yours. You can also request information about screening/evaluation services, which each state is required to have in place. For two-year-olds, look for your county or state's "Early Intervention Program for Infants and Toddlers"; for three-to-five-year olds, you can contact the special education specialist in your local public school district or call your local elementary school.

Your concerns may also lead you to do some research yourself. You can read about developmental delays and disabilities, contact organizations that can give you information about services and testing, and/or seek professional help on your own. If you have a child with diagnosed disabilities or other special concerns, you need specific information about your entitlements under federal law. In either case, you can start by contacting the organizations and Web sites listed in appendixes E and F.

On the other hand, you may be concerned that, because your child's program includes children with specific disabilities who require special attention, the teacher cannot accommodate the special needs children along with your child. One of the best ways to address this concern initially is to visit your child's preschool program. There you will see for yourself how well the children are attended to, both individually and as a group.

Any responses to these concerns are complex and depend on many variables. Although a child with a disability often requires specialized support, a classroom atmosphere that emphasizes a respect for differences and values each person's ability to make a contribution can work well for all children—if, and only if, appropriate support services are available.

Specialized Programs for Children with Special Needs

Under the Individuals with Disabilities Education Act of 1990 (IDEA),[16] intervention services for children with disabilities are available from birth. Children eligible for services include those with a wide range of developmental delays, children with vision or hearing problems, cerebral palsy, autism, mental retardation, or profound multiple disabilities.

Children from birth to age three fall under Part C of the act and are eligible for early intervention services. These services may include speech, occupational, and physical therapies, as well as educational and psychological services. At age three, children transition into Part B, which is coordinated by local school districts. In many districts, the only preschool programs available may be Part B special education classrooms. In addition to playing an important role in children's social and emotional development, these special education programs (which are free for children with diagnosed disabilities) provide speech, physical, and occupational therapies based on each child's needs.

It is important to note that early intervention programs for infants and toddlers and preschool special education programs are governed by two different sets of federal regulations under the IDEA–Part C and Part B respectively. Not only are the regulations for Parts C and B different, but each program has a different focus. Early intervention programs focus primarily on the child and family and emphasize family and developmental priorities. Preschool special education programs have an educational focus and emphasize the child's educational needs.

Another resource is the local Head Start program. Head Start is a federally funded program that offers comprehensive services–including high-quality early childhood education, nutrition, health, and social services–to low-income children. All Head Start programs are required to reserve at least 10 percent of their enrollment for children with disabilities, and they frequently have slots available, even for children who do not meet the income eligibility criteria.

Many parents of children with special needs are able to take advantage of the "best of both worlds"–receiving services from their school system and enrolling their children in high-quality developmentally appropriate preschool programs. When children with disabilities are part of regular preschool classrooms, this is called "inclusion."

Inclusion of Children with Special Needs into Preschool Programs

Throughout this book, we stress the importance of social and emotional development. For children with disabilities, this emphasis is even more important, because they may be at greater risk for delays in these areas than are nondisabled children. Some research shows that children with special needs do better academically and socially when they are taught in regular classrooms instead of separate settings.[17] Research also indicates that benefits for other children may include learning to understand and appreciate diversity, gaining a better understanding for the needs of others, and learning to feel comfortable being around people different from themselves.[18] As a matter of philosophy, many quality preschools are committed to including children with disabilities in their programs. In addition, as more school districts add prekindergarten programs, inclusion will most likely become increasingly prevalent. You should understand, however, that for inclusion to work well for all children, teachers need additional classroom support and the advice of experts.

Making Inclusion Work for the Child with a Disability

Fortunately, the two key components of high-quality early childhood programs—understanding child development and individualizing the program based on each child's developmental profile—make inclusion of a child with a disability much less daunting than it might appear. In the simplest terms, teachers need to do for special needs children what they do for all children, perhaps only to a greater extent.

If you have a child with a disability in a mainstream classroom, there are several things you can do to help your child succeed. Before the school year begins, schedule a meeting with the school's director, your child's teachers, and any therapists or special educators with whom you work. The purpose of these meetings is to ensure that the teachers understand the nature of your child's disability and your goals for the year. Every child who is classified with a disability has a formal set of goals—either an Individualized Family Service Plan (IFSP, for two-year-olds) or an Individualized Education Program (IEP, for three-year-olds and up). While these goals are developed for federal or state programs, they are also useful tools for the mainstream classroom. For instance, teachers want to know how important it is that they work on your child's physical therapy goals: Is that your primary concern, or would you rather that teachers focus on social and emotional development?

You may want to schedule regular meetings among yourself, your child's therapists, and teachers throughout the year to consider issues that arise and to train teachers to best meet your child's needs. Often, simple adaptations to the environment (such as a special chair) or to toys (such as knobs on puzzle pieces) can make a world of difference in the child's ability to participate fully with the other children in the classroom. Sometimes the adaptations will be more significant, such as needing an extra aide in the classroom. Remember, however, that because preschool teachers do not typically have a special education or physical therapy background, ongoing communication among team members will be vital to ensure that your child receives the preschool experience he or she deserves.

Making Inclusion Work for the Nondisabled Child

If your child is in a classroom with a child or children with disabilities or other special concerns, you may want to find out more about the support services available to assist the teacher. For example, if the child with a disability receives assistance from an additional adult in the classroom, all children are likely to benefit from the lower student/teacher ratio. On the other hand, if the necessary support is not available, all children can suffer.

While recognizing the family's right to privacy, you may want to encourage the family of the child with a disability to talk with you, other parents, and the children in the class about their child's strengths as well as the nature of the disability. With the parents' involvement, you can learn what the school and the teacher are doing to support the child and what you and your child can do to help.

It is very important to remember that the child with special needs is still just a child who is more similar to than different from other children. In fact, during the preschool years, children do not generally comment on other children's disabilities. You may be amazed to find that your child's best friend is the girl in the wheelchair or the boy who uses a cane or wears special glasses. This type of respect and appreciation for people who are different may be the most important benefit your child receives from an inclusive classroom.

– APPENDIX C –
Checklists

Screening Phone Call

Name of Program _____

Director _____

Address _____

Phone Number _____

Tell me about your educational philosophy. _____

_____

_____

What is your admissions process? _____

_____

What are the tuition, registration, and other fees? _____

_____

What are your hours and calendar year? _____

_____

Do you offer child care before and after the regular program day
(extended hours)? _____

_____

Do you have a summer program? _____

_____

Do you have a kindergarten program? _____

_____

What is your illness or sick child policy? _____

_____

What are your discipline policies? _____

_____

_____

What is your policy on including children with special needs or disabilities? _____

_____

Are you registered or licensed by the state? _____

_____

Are you accredited by NAEYC or any other accrediting body?

_____

What is the child/staff ratio?* How does that compare with the state licensing regulations? _____

_____

What is the total group size of the class?   _____

_____

How long have your teachers been with the program? (The national annual turnover rate in child care is 30 percent for teachers and even higher for assistant teachers. The lower the turnover rate, the better a relationship your child is likely to form with a teacher.)

_____

_____

_____

* For two-year-olds, 12/2; three-year-olds, 16/2; four-and five-year-olds, 20/2. These figures are from *Accreditation Criteria Procedures of the National Academy of Early Childhood Programs* (Washington, DC: NAEYC, 1991).

What are the educational requirements for your teachers and teacher assistants or aides? _____

_____

What are your policies about the food served to children? _____

_____

What kinds of activities do children do during the day? _____

_____

Can you give me an example of the daily schedule? _____

_____

How do teachers communicate with parents? _____

_____

Are parents welcome to visit when they wish? _____

_____

How are parents involved? _____

_____

_____

Do you require written permission to release children to someone other than the person regularly authorized to pick them up at the end of the day? _____

_____

When You Visit

Name of Program _____

Director _____

Address _____

Phone Number _____

Date of Visit _____

Overall Impressions

	yes	no
• Do children appear happy and engaged with one another and with teachers?	___	___
• Are the teachers interacting with children in a nurturing way?	___	___
• Do the classrooms and outdoor areas appear bright, cheerful, clean, safe, and well maintained?	___	___
• Do you think your child could be happy here?	___	___
• Will you be happy with your child here?	___	___

Comments _____

_____

_____

_____

Health and Safety

• Are the classrooms and outdoor areas free from conditions that might cause accidents?	___	___
• Are materials and equipment in good repair?	___	___
• Are children well supervised at all times?	___	___
• Are there written procedures for dealing with emergencies such as fires and accidents?	___	___
• Are the classrooms well lit and ventilated?	___	___

Comments _____

_____

_____

_____

Physical Environment	yes	no
• Are interest areas set up for children to select materials and plan activities?	___	___
• Are materials on low shelves labeled with pictures or words so children can reach what they need and replace items when they are finished?	___	___
• Are there enough materials and duplicates of popular toys?	___	___
• Do children have space to store their belongings?	___	___
• Does the child/adult ratio correspond to what you were told during the screening phone call?	___	___
• Do you see books and writing materials available?	___	___
• Do you see signs and labels around the room, the alphabet posted at children's eye level, printed children's names used for a purpose?	___	___
• Do you see a variety of children's work displayed rather than mostly adult made art?	___	___
• Do you see evidence of group problem-solving activities such as graphs, charts, pattern designs, estimation experiments?	___	___

Comments _____

_____

_____

_____

The Schedule

	yes	no
• Is there a schedule posted in the classroom?	___	___
• Does the schedule offer times for active and quiet play?	___	___
• Is time allowed for children to select their own activities and to play for an extended period?	___	___
• Does the schedule include one or two periods (of thirty to forty-five minutes each) outdoors each day?	___	___

Comments _____

_____

_____

_____

Teachers

	yes	no
• Do teachers respond to children's questions and requests and call children by name?	___	___
• Do teachers respond quickly and positively to children's needs and questions, comfort distressed children, and help them deal with problems constructively?	___	___
• Do teachers bend, kneel, or sit down to establish close contact when talking with children?	___	___
• Do teachers engage children in interesting conversations?	___	___
• Do teachers describe the behavior they want to see in positive terms: "Keep the water inside the water table. The floor gets slippery if it's wet."?	___	___
• Do teachers plan activities that involve children in cooperative efforts and encourage children to work together and help each other?	___	___

	yes	no

- Do teachers coach children who have difficulty finding a way to play with other children? (This includes working with children who may be shy or excitable.)
- Do teachers praise and encourage children?

Comments _____

_____

_____

_____

Children

- Do you see children playing alone and in small groups with a variety of materials?
- Do children look happy and engaged with one another and with adults?
- Are children talking as they play together?
- Are children engaged in self-initiated or teacher-planned activities in which they use physical skills such as hopping, skipping, jumping, throwing and catching, striking, and balancing?
- Do children seem interested in language and literacy activities such as looking at books, writing signs and stories, dictating stories, and expressing their ideas?
- Do you see children engaged in activities that involve mathematical thinking, such as measuring ingredients for a baking project or organizing objects according to a system?
- Are children using concrete or manipulative materials to explore shapes and numbers and to measure objects?

	yes	no
• Do you see evidence that children are engaged in scientific explorations, such as observing a pet, planting seeds and examining them with a magnifier, comparing objects?	——	——
• Do you see children using scientific tools and equipment to investigate—magnifying devices, eye droppers, measuring cups, magnets, gears, string and other objects for measuring?	——	——
• Do children treat adults and each other respectfully, showing an awareness of classroom rules and taking responsibility for the classroom by putting things away at cleanup time?	——	——
• Do you see older preschoolers working together on projects, such as making a mural, planning an event, or recreating the neighborhood in the block area?	——	——
• Are teachers engaging children in a variety of activities outdoors?	——	——
• Do you see children using a variety of art media?		
• Do children handle art materials and other classroom supplies purposefully and clean up when they are finished?	——	——
• Are children engaged in moving to music, listening to music, or making up their own songs?	——	——

Comments _____

_____

_____

_____

– APPENDIX D –
For Further Reading

You should be able to find these resources in your local library or bookstore. The books listed with an asterisk are available for purchase online at Teaching Strategies' Web site: http://www.TeachingStrategies.com.

Beyond Discipline: From Compliance to Community. Alfie Kohn. Alexandria, VA: Association for Supervision and Curriculum Development, 1996.

Child Care That Works: A Parent's Guide to Finding Quality Child Care. Eva and Mon Cochran. New York: Houghton Mifflin, 1997.

The Creative Curriculum® for Early Childhood, Third Edition. Diane Trister Dodge and Laura J. Colker. Washington, DC: Teaching Strategies, 1992.*

Developmentally Appropriate Practice in Early Childhood Programs, Revised Edition. Sue Bredekamp and Carol Copple, editors. Washington, DC: National Association for the Education of Young Children, 1997.*

Emotional Intelligence: Why It Can Matter More Than IQ. Daniel Goleman. New York: Bantam Books, 1995.*

Frames of Mind: The Theory of Multiple Intelligences. Howard Gardner. New York: BasicBooks, 1983.*

The Growth of the Mind and the Endangered Origins of Intelligence. Stanley I. Greenspan. New York: Addison-Wesley, 1997.*

The Hurried Child: Growing Up Too Fast Too Soon. David Elkind. New York: Addison-Wesley, 1988.*

Kindergarten: It Isn't What It Used to Be. Susan K. Golant and Mitch Golant. Los Angeles: Lowell House, 1997.*

Miseducation: Preschoolers at Risk. David Elkind. New York: Alfred A. Knopf, 1987.*

Punished by Rewards: The Trouble with Gold Stars, Incentive Plans, A's, Praise, and Other Bribes. Alfie Kohn. New York: Houghton Mifflin, 1993.*

Smart Moves: Why Learning Is Not All in Your Head. Carla Hannaford. Arlington, VA: Great Ocean, 1995.*

Smart Start: The Parents' Complete Guide to Preschool Education. Marian Edelman Borden. New York: Facts on File, 1997.

Your Child's Growing Mind: A Practical Guide to Brain Development and Learning from Birth to Adolescence. Jane M. Healy. New York: Doubleday, 1994.*

Special Needs and Inclusion

The Child with Special Needs. Stanley I. Greenspan and Serena Wieder. New York: Addison-Wesley, 1998.*

Exceptional Parent Magazine. PO Box 3000, Dept. EP, Danville, NJ 07834 (1-800-247-8080).

Negotiating the Special Education Maze: A Guide for Parents and Teachers, Third Edition. Winifred Anderson, Stephen Chitwood, and Deidre Hayden. Bethesda, MD: Woodbine House, 1997.*

– APPENDIX E –
National Organizations and Information Clearinghouses

Organizations

Center for the Child Care Workforce

733 15th Street, N.W., Suite 800
Washington, DC 20005
Phone: (202) 737-7700

CCW is a nonprofit resource and advocacy organization committed to improving the quality of child care services through upgrading the compensation and training of child care teachers and providers. CCW serves as the national coordinator of the Worthy Wage Campaign, a grassroots effort to empower child care workers themselves to fight for solutions to the staffing crisis.

Child Care Action Campaign

330 7th Avenue, 17th Floor
New York, NY 10001
Phone: (212) 239-0138
Web site: http://www.usakids.org/sites/ccac.html

CCAC is a national advocacy organization that works to stimulate and support the development of policies and programs that increase the availability of quality affordable child care.

Child Care Aware

Hotline: 1-800-424-2246

Child Care Aware is a national initiative designed to improve the quality of child care and increase the availability of high-quality child care in local communities. Child Care Aware operates a toll-free hotline for parents seeking child care information and assistance, provides a link to child care resource and referral agencies nationwide, and offers free information to parents on choosing high-quality child care.

Children's Defense Fund

25 E Street, NW
Washington, DC 20001
Phone: (202) 628-8787
Web site: http://www.childrensdefense.org

CDF is a nonprofit research and advocacy organization that exists to provide a strong and effective voice for children. It pays particular attention to the needs of poor, minority, and disabled children. CDF's goal is to educate the nation about the needs of children and encourage preventative investment in children before they get sick, drop out of school, or get into trouble.

The Children's Foundation

725 15th Street, NW, #505
Washington, DC 20005
Phone: (202) 347-3300

The Children's Foundation is a private, national educational, nonprofit organization that strives to improve the lives of children and those who care for them. Through the National Child Care Advocacy Project and National Child Support Project, the Children's Foundation conducts research and provides information and training on federal food programs, quality child care, leadership development, health care, and enforcement of court-ordered child support.

Ecumenical Child Care Network

8765 West Higgins Road, Suite 405
Chicago, IL 60631
Phone: (312) 693-4040

The Ecumenical Child Care Network is a national Christian interdenominational membership organization whose members advocate for high-quality, equitable, and affordable child care and education in churches and other religious organizations. It challenges members to apply anti-bias/anti-racist principles in their work and in all that they do.

Families and Work Institute

330 Seventh Avenue, 14th Floor
New York, NY 10001
Phone: (212) 465-2044
Web site: http://www.familiesandworkinst.org

The Families and Work Institute is a nonprofit research and planning organization committed to developing new approaches for balancing the changing needs of America's families with the continuing need for workplace productivity. The Institute conducts policy research on a broad range of issues related to the changing demographics of the work force and operates a national clearinghouse on work and family life.

National Association for the Education of Young Children (NAEYC)

1509 16th Street, NW
Washington, DC 20036
Phone: 1-800-424-2460 or (202) 232-8777
Web site: http://www.naeyc.org

NAEYC is a nonprofit professional organization of more than one hundred thousand members dedicated to improving the quality of care and education provided to young children. The Association administers the National Academy of Early Childhood Programs, a voluntary national accreditation system for high-quality early childhood programs. You can search for accredited programs by city and zip code on NAEYC's Web site.

National Association for Family Child Care (NAFCC)

206 6th Avenue, Suite 900
Des Moines, IA 50309-4018
Phone: 1-800-359-3817 or (515) 282-8192
Fax: (515) 282-9117
E-mail: nafcc@assoc-mgmt.com
Web site: http://www.nafcc.org/

NAFCC is a national membership organization that works with the more than four hundred state and local family child care provider associations in the United States. The focus of NAFCC is to promote quality family child care through accreditation and to promote training and leadership development through specialized technical assistance.

National Association of Child Care Resource and Referral Agencies (NACCRRA)

1319 F Street, NW, Suite 810
Washington, DC 20004-1106
Phone: (202) 393-5501
Web site: http://www.childcarerr.org

NACCRRA is a national membership organization of over four hundred community child care resource and referral agencies in all fifty states. NACCRRA's mission is to promote the growth and development of high-quality resource and referral services and to exercise leadership to build a diverse, high-quality child care system with parental choice and equal access for all families.

National Black Child Development Institute

1023 Fifteenth Street, NW, Suite 600
Washington, DC 20005
Phone: (202) 387-1281
Web site: http://www.nbcdi.org

NBCDI is a national nonprofit organization that serves as a critical resource for improving the quality of life of African-American children, youth, and families through direct services, public education programs, leadership training, and research.

National Child Care Association

1016 Rosser Street
Conyers, GA 30207
Phone: 1-800-543-7161
E-mail: nccallw@mindspring.com
Web site: http://www.nccanet.org/

The National Child Care Association (NCCA) is a professional trade association representing the private, licensed early childhood care and education community. NCCA has a dual advocacy for quality, affordable child care as well as the business of child care.

National Head Start Association

1651 Prince Street
Alexandria, VA 22314
Phone: (703) 739-0875
Web site: http://www.nhsa.org

NHSA is the membership organization representing Head Start parents, staff, directors, and friends across the nation. NHSA focuses on issues that shape the future of Head Start and uses its national voice to inform communities, states, corporate America, and Washington lawmakers.

National Indian Child Care Association

279 East 137th Street
Glenpool, OK 74033
Phone: (918) 756-2112

The purpose of the National Indian Child Care Association is to advocate for quality child care for Native American children, to disseminate information, and to build trust and communication between Native American Tribes to perpetuate the identification and consideration of Tribal needs.

National Jewish Early Childhood Network (NJECN)

11 Wonder View Court
North Potomac, MD 20878
Phone: (301) 279-7505
E-mail: LAINEYG@aol.com

NJECN consists of Jewish early childhood directors and teachers throughout the United States and Canada who are concerned with the special issues and concerns of your Jewish children. Through a variety of tours, speakers, and workshops, the members of the Network share resources, curriculum ideas, and philosophical approaches.

Information Clearinghouses

ERIC Clearinghouse on Disabilities and Gifted Education

Council for Exceptional Children
1920 Association Drive
Reston, VA 20191-1589
Phone: 1-800-328-0272
E-mail: ericec@cec.sped.org
Web site: http://www.cec.sped.org

ERIC Clearinghouse on Elementary and Early Childhood Education

University of Illinois at Urbana-Champaign
Children's Research Center
51 Gerty Drive
Champaign, IL 61820-7469
Phone: 1-800-583-4135 or (217) 333-1386
Web site: http://ericeece.org

National Child Care Information Center

301 Maple Avenue West
Suite 602
Vienna, VA 22180
Phone: 1-800-616-2242
E-mail: agoldstein@acf.dhhs.gov
Web site: http://nccic.org

National Clearinghouse on Families and Youth

PO Box 13505
Silver Spring, MD 20911-3505
Phone: (301) 608-8098

National Information Center for Children and Youth with Disabilities

PO Box 1492
Washington, DC 20013-1492
Phone: 1-800-695-0285
E-mail: nichcy@aed.org
Web site: http://www.nichcy.org/

APPENDIX F
World Wide Web Sites

Here is a brief listing of some World Wide Web sites that deal with parenting and preschool education issues. This list is by no means exhaustive, and new sites pop up every day. A great place to begin is at our site—http://www.TeachingStrategies.com—where you'll find links to all of these other sites plus an online bookshop where you can order many of the books referred to in the resource section. In addition, we host weekly chat sessions and monitor bulletin boards as part of our partnership with Parent Soup (http://www.parentsoup.com/edcentral). Have fun exploring—you'll find statistics, articles, resources, organizations, activities you can do with your children, books, and a lot more!

Parent Involvement in Education

Child Care Aware	http://www.childcarerr.org/childcareaware
Family Web Corner	http://www.nauticom.net/www/cokids/
Family.com	http://family.disney.com/Categories/Education/
Kidsource	http://www.kidsource.com
National Parent Information Network	http://www.npin.org

Parent Soup's Education Central	http://www.parentsoup.com/edcentral
Teaching Strategies	http://www.TeachingStrategies.com
Watoto World	http://www.melanet.com/watoto/ watoto.html

Children's Literature and Software

Children's Software Revue	http://www2.childrenssoftware.com/ childrenssoftware/
Gryphon House (activity books and children's literature)	http://www.ghbooks.com/children

Education Links, Advocacy

Children's Defense Fund	http://www.childrensdefense.org
ERIC Clearinghouse on Elementary and Early Childhood Education	http://ericeece.org
Kids Campaigns	http://www.kidscampaigns.org
National Child Care Information Center	http://nccic.org
National Network for Child Care	http://www.nncc.org
Stand for Children	http://www.stand.org/

Special Needs

ERIC Clearinghouse on Disabilities and Gifted Education (The Council for Exceptional Children)	http://www.cec.sped.org
Family Village	http://familyvillage.wisc.edu
Federation for Children with Special Needs	http://www.fcsn.org
National Association for Gifted Children	http://www.nagc.org
National Information Center for Children and Youth with Disabilities	http://www.nichcy.org

National Organizations

National Association for Family Child Care (NAFCC)	http://www.nafcc.org
National Association for the Education of Young Children (NAEYC) (search for accredited centers in your area)	http://www.naeyc.org
National Association of Child Care Resource and Referral Agencies (NACCRRA)	http://www.childcarerr.org
National Black Child Development Institute	http://www.nbcdi.org
National Head Start Association	http://www.nhsa.org

Endnotes

1. D. C. Burts, C. H. Hart, R. Charlesworth, and L. Kirk, "A Comparison of Frequencies of Stress Behaviors Observed in Kindergarten Children in Classrooms with Developmentally Appropriate Versus Developmentally Inappropriate Instructional Practices," *Early Childhood Research Quarterly* 5 (1992): 407–23.

2. D. Stipek, R. Feiler, and D. Daniels, "Effects of Different Instructional Approaches on Young Children's Achievement and Motivation," *Child Development* 66 (1995): 209–23.

3. R. A. Marcon, "Differential Effects of Three Preschool Models on Inner-City Four-Year-Olds," *Early Childhood Research Quarterly* 7 (1992): 517–30.

4. K. Hirsh-Pasek, M. C. Hyson, and L. Rescorla, "Academic Environments in Preschool: Do They Pressure or Challenge Young Children?" *Early Education and Development* 1 (1990): 401–23.

5. Sara Smilansky and Leah Shefatya, *Facilitating Play: A Medium for Promoting Cognitive, Socio-Emotional and Academic Development in Young Children* (Gaithersburg, MD: Psychosocial and Educational Publications, 1990), 1–3.

6. J. E. Johnson, "The Role of Play in Cognitive Development," in *Children's Play and Learning: Perspectives and Policy Implications*, edited by E. Klugman and S. Smilansky (New York: Teachers College Press, 1990).

7. Carla Hannaford, *Smart Moves: Why Learning Is Not All in Your Head* (Arlington, VA: Great Ocean Publishers, 1995); Shore, Rima. *Rethinking the Brain: New Insights into Early Development* (New York: Families and Work Institute, 1997).

8. Howard Gardner, *Multiple Intelligences: The Theory in Practice* (New York: Basic Books, 1993).

9. Daniel Goleman, *Emotional Intelligence: Why It Can Matter More Than IQ* (New York: Bantam Books, 1995).

10. A. D. Pellegrini and C. D. Glickman, "Measuring Kindergartners' Social Competence," *Young Children* 45 (April 1990): 40–44.

11. Sue Bredekamp and Carol Copple, eds., *Developmentally Appropriate Practice in Early Childhood Programs*, rev. ed. (Washington, DC: National Association for the Education of Young Children, 1997), 98.

12. Johanne T. Peck, Ginny McCaig, and Mary Ellen Sapp, *Kindergarten Policies: What Is Best for Children?*, vol. 2 (Washington, DC: Research Monographs of National Association for the Education of Young Children, 1988), 31.

13. Sam Meisels, "Assessing Readiness," paper prepared for The Synthesis Conference on the transition to kindergarten, National Center for Early Development and Learning (Charlottesville, VA: February 1998).

14. Johanne T. Peck, Ginny McCaig, and Mary Ellen Sapp, *Kindergarten Policies: What Is Best for Children?*, vol. 2 (Washington, DC: Research Monographs of National Association for the Education of Young Children, 1988), 17.

15. John M. Love, J. Lawrence Abner, and Jeanne Brooks-Gunn, *Strategies for Assessing Community Progress Toward Achieving the First National Educational Goal* (Princeton, NJ: Policy Research, Inc., 1994), 19.

16. *Individuals with Disabilities Education Act*, P.L. 101-476 (1990). The IDEA was amended in 1997.

17. J. Nisbet, *Education Reform: Summary and Recommendations: The National Reform Agenda and People with Mental retardation: Putting People First* (Washington, DC: U.S. Department of Health and Human Services, 1994).

18. D. Staub and C. A. Peck, "What Are the Outcomes for Nondisabled Students?" *Educational Leadership* 52 (April 1994): 36–40.23. D. Staub and C.A. Peck, "What Are the Outcomes for Nondisabled Students," *Educational Leadership* 52:4 (1994): 36-40.

Index

Notes

Notes

A Note from
Teaching Strategies, Inc.

Do you want to hear more? Teaching Strategies has a national network of experienced educators who work with directors, teachers, family child care providers, and parents to bring about the types of preschool classrooms advocated in this book. The authors and these expert facilitators are available as speakers and workshop leaders for preschool staff development and parent workshops.

Join Us at the Soup!

Teaching Strategies has formed a partnership with Parent Soup—a leading parenting site on the Internet—to present Education Central. Education Central is a new area of Parent Soup designed to answer your questions about your child's education, from preschool through high school, and to put you in touch with experts and other parents.

Diane Trister Dodge and Toni Bickart conduct weekly live chat sessions and monitor bulletin board discussions as part of Education Central. To chat live with either author, go to America Online (keyword: ParentSoup) or www.parentsoup.com/edcentral. We would love to hear from you about your child's experiences in preschool. We hope to meet you there!

To Contact Us:

Diane Trister Dodge/Toni Bickart
Teaching Strategies, Inc.
P.O. Box 42243
Washington, DC 20015
(800) 637-3652
Email: info@TeachingStrategies.com
http://www.TeachingStrategies.com

About the Authors

Diane Trister Dodge, President of Teaching
Strategies, Inc., has been a leader in the field
of early childhood education for thirty-five
years. She is the author of more than twenty
books, including *The Creative Curriculum®* for
Early Childhood, the country's second most
used preschool model, and *A Parent's Guide to
Early Childhood Education*, which has sold in

excess of 600,000 copies. She holds a master's degree in Early
Childhood Education from the Bank Street College of Education and
began her career as a preschool and kindergarten teacher. In 1966,
Diane helped set up a Head Start program in rural Mississippi. She is
a well-known speaker and trainer and a former member of the
Governing Board of the National Association for the Education of
Young Children (NAEYC). She is the parent of three children.

Toni Bickart was a teacher at The Sidwell
Friends School in Washington, D.C., and is
a Senior Associate at Teaching Strategies,
Inc. She served as a teacher mentor in a
multi-year program with the D.C. Public
Schools and presents workshops for teachers
and parents around the country. She is the
co-author (with Diane Trister Dodge and
Judy Jablon) of *What Every Parent Needs to
Know About 1st, 2nd & 3rd Grades* and

Constructing Curriculum for the Primary Grades, a resource for teachers. In addition to her educational background, Toni holds a master's degree in Social Work from Columbia University. She is the parent of two children.

Teaching Strategies believes that the future of our country depends on our ability to nurture the optimal growth and development of every child. High-quality early childhood programs develop strong partnerships with families to build the foundation children need to become enthusiastic life-long learners who succeed in school and in life. The mission of Teaching Strategies, Inc., is to enhance the quality of early childhood programs by offering the highest quality curriculum materials, training programs, parenting resources, and staff develop-ment services that are practical, developmentally appropriate, respon-sive to the needs of the field, and reflect the most innovative thinking.

Also by Teaching Strategies

What's next after preschool and Kindergarten? For you and your grade schoolers, *What Every Parent Needs to Know About 1st, 2nd & 3rd Grades* takes you inside exciting classrooms where children are challenged to become thinkers, problem-solvers and enthusiastic learners. This terrific resource will show you what should happen in your child's classroom, and help you make the most of your child's grade school experience.

"This clear and concise book shows how children learn and care-fully guides parents through the essential elements they should look for in their child's early elementary school experience."
    —Marian Wright Edelman, President, Children's Defense Fund

What Every Parent Needs to Know About 1st, 2nd & 3rd Grades
by Toni S. Bickart, Diane Trister Dodge and Judy R. Jablon
$12.95 U.S.; ISBN 1-57071-156-9

Available at Bookstores Everywhere or Call 800-432-7444!